ENDORSEMENTS

By His Stripes, promises to be an open read for those who have experienced the pains of sexual abuse. Christina's ability to tell a captivating story of faith, love, and the healing power of a faithful God will inspire readers to face their difficult past, as they take their own journey to heal. Christina's story reads like a novel with plots and twists, which leaves the reader desiring more of her story. I've had the remarkable privilege to witness Christina's transformation from a wounded, fragile woman to a woman of purpose and promise. *By His Stripes* lifted the hopes of a desperate woman seeking what she had heard others testify about the goodness of Jesus, to now becoming a woman that knows all about His scares that heal. I see Christina now as she holds her head up high and smiles with that yes, Jesus is a healer smile. *By His Stripes* was truly written for a time such as now.

Pastor Gwendolyn Scott
TrueWay Apostolic Ministries
Apex, North Carolina

Christina Mial is an awesome woman of God with a beautiful smile that lights up a room. Her life is a testimony that God is a protector and a keeper. Although she has faced numerous obstacles, God's amazing grace covered her and brought her through victoriously. Her strong faith in God and unwavering perseverance gives me hope and encourages me to never give up as I continue this race. Sexual abuse is detrimental to the human's soul. Statistics showed one in four girls and one in seven boys are victimized by the age of 18. As a victim of sexual abuse, I know from experience the effects of this evil sin and how it can shape one's life forever. By His Stripes pulls back the curtains on sexual abuse, and Christina reveals how sexual abuse shaped her life as a child, adolescent, and adult. Through her wisdom, she shares painful experiences of her past, BUT she shares the awesome revelation of God's power and faithfulness. This book is a must read. It will provide hope to the readers and is destined to set the captives free.

Ms. Katrina L. Sweet, Rocky Mount, NC
Author of Silent Screams from Within

.. It makes you want to start reading right away to find out what happened. It is the guilty look into a person's life... When you know you have NO BUSINESS SEEING THEIR PAIN.... But you want to STAY IN THEIR COMPANY to somehow help EASE THE HURT. This book seems to KEEP YOU ON YOUR TOES while SITTING YOU BACK DOWN because the joy seemed to be for only a minute... Until you see that the true joy still came in the morning. All in short of this I get all the length of who you are... Have came to be.. And who you will soon become.

Corneal Sevyn "Seven" Johnson
New Oreleans, Louisiana
Motivational Speaker
www.quinspirations.com

By His Stripes

DEDICATION

This book is dedicated to all of the little Christina's in the world. I love you!

Christina L. Mial

TABLE OF CONTENTS

	PREFACE	9
1	CHRISTINA'S WORLD	15
2	CHRISTINA'S CHILDHOOD	20
3	CHRISTINA'S EXPERIENCES	28
4	CHRISTINA'S PARENTS	33
5	CHRISTINA'S HURTS	38
6	CHRISTINA'S NEW ADVENTURE	44
7	CHRISTINA MOVES…. AGAIN	54
8	CHRISTINA'S PAIN	63
9	CHRISTINA'S PAIN CONTINUES…	71
10	CHRISTINA'S REJECTION	82
11	CHRISTINA'S WHIRLWIND	94
12	CHRISTINA'S SPIRAL	112
13	CHRISTINA'S SEARCH	127
14	CHRISTINA'S REDEMPTION	141
	EPILOGUE	146

ACKNOWLEDGEMENTS 155

OTHER VALUABLE INFORMATION

Preface

Just a Moment of Your Time

I just wanted to share why this particular book was written and why it was written the way it is. First, I wanted to share with you the details of my journey and I wanted you to know I was talking to you. Granted I am telling my story but it is also me inviting you into my living room, to sit on my couch, and hear what I experienced that ended with these pages now being in your hand.

I wrote this book with the broken in mind. God reminded me of the pain I carried for years and showed me the faces of many that carry the same pain. The pages of this book were written with the ones in mind afraid to speak out. For the mothers and fathers seeking answers as to why their child may be acting out, this book is for you. For the person that is ashamed of the weight of dirty secrets, I pray that you will find release in this book. Someone somewhere is reading this and has decided that the mistakes they have made have already predestined them for a failed life.

My prayer is also that after reading this it will be recognized that the only failure is in giving up. No matter who we are or what we've done, the moment we choose to believe in and trust God's plan for our lives we change the future. It is at that moment that every bad thing we have ever done and that has ever been done to us can be used for the good of God and to His glory. As Genesis 50:20 tells us when Joseph's brothers were worried about him getting revenge for how they had treated him, he responded, "You intended to harm me, but God intended it for good to accomplish what is now being done, the saving of many lives." This scripture speaks dearly to my life and I know to the lives of many other victims of abuse that now choose to speak out. Our abusers have the intent to control us and to break us but once we are free of their hold on our lives and we help someone else, we too are saving many lives as Joseph speaks about in this verse.

One of the main issues that haunted my conscience that I had was that of promiscuity. I was convinced because of the past sexual history I had experienced, I was forever going to be damaged goods. Society after all teaches us that no man wants a loose woman while at the same time every time we turn on the television it is forcing sex down our throats. Again, I read of someone in the Bible with a dirty past that God still used. In the book of Joshua we are introduced to Rahab.

Rahab was a well-known prostitute that chose to trust God's plan and believed that included even her. Despite her past and despite what people were saying about her, she risked her life and hid two spies in her home when they came. This noble act set her up in the bloodline to be an ancestor of our Lord and Savior Jesus Christ. Rahab's story taught me that not only can

God use anybody but He will also use them to accomplish great things. Rahab did not let her fear stop her from believing God would deliver on His every word and promise to her.

When I first heard the Holy Spirit telling me I was going to write, it was not during a time where I was ready to receive it. As time went on and I would share things I had been through in my life with people, they too would tell me to write a book. In the beginning of my literary journey, this started off as just a book. I realize now that it never worked out where it was published because it was not time. Although God had shown me the promise, the path that would lead me to completing it would still have to be taken. I did try to write in my own might. I had journals on top of journals written of what I was going through. I even tried to write it as an urban novel depicting real life situations and people as fictional places and characters. This was not what I was to do; this is not what I was told to do.

Later in life, again I heard God tell me to write. This time, I heard the Lord say, ***"Tell your story"***. By the time this was dropped in my spirit again, not only had I been through a whole lot more but I was at a different place in life. I am at a different place in life. Yet and still, I was not trying to revisit the pain of those midnight hours. I started to question God. I was asking Him why now? "I am saved now God", I would tell Him. "How can I write a book now and tell the story of the things that I went through as they happened and I know longer have the same profane mouth that I did when it happened?" Question after question I asked God instead of just doing what He told me to do which was just to write.

Eventually I did start. First I started off with blogs and getting my feet wet with sharing intimate details of me on the social media networks. The more I wrote the more therapeutic it was. The more I wrote the more God revealed not only what He had done for me but what He was doing with me and through me. People from all over were responding and sharing their stories as well of being survivors of abuse and some of the things that I talked about. God also started showing me how there was a revelation of Him in everyday life. I was complaining less and less and starting to speak life over my situations more.

Now the story clearly isn't over and things have yet to be seen what He is doing in my life, but I can say this. I have discovered that without Him I am nothing. God took me to a place where I had no one to depend on and to call on but Him. Even after He healed me from all of the things that you are about to read about in this book, I still experienced some painful situations but the difference was He was right there with me.

So, as you take this trip through my life with me, again, I pray that you are touched by the things I experienced but not saddened by the hardships I lived. This book is to introduce you to my God. **Jehovah Jireh**, My Provider. I want you to know **Jehovah Nissi**, a God that will be a banner of protection around you even when you do not realize it. I am introducing God as

Jehovah Rohi, My Shepherd. The same God that we read about in Psalm 23 is the same one that guides me today. But most importantly and certainly not the last, I want you to know ***Jehovah Shammah***. This name means God is there. This name means so much to me because this was the name that I later learned to describe Him as the One who is there.

The door that God has me opening up for you is not one that I walked through easily. Before these pages were even printed there was a war that I had to fight and I know I will still have to fight because that is just what happens in ministry. Opposition. I also know that even in that, He opened the door for this and I trust that it was not to leave me out in the cold alone. Even with this book, I had no idea how I was going to pay for the publishing fees. I was coming up with all kinds of fundraisers and networking trying to figure out how I could get it done. Again, I was in the way. God told me to do it so should I have not remembered that He had already provided a way for it to be done?

The publishing of this book is the result of a national contest in which Shifting a Generation Publishing offered aspiring authors the opportunity to have their books published at the expense of the publishing company. Yours truly won second place. I know that was no one but God. I entered the contest at the last minute after it had been ran for the summer. I literally paid the entry fee on the last day. Then I waited. In the process of waiting, I did not worry. Well, you are reading the end result. God knew I did not have the money it would take to have my book published and He provided a way for me to have it done. How could I not trust Him with where so ever this leads me? His hand has been on me and this project from day one. Thank you for sharing this season with me.

Be blessed.

Christina

Chapter One
Christina's World

The world was introduced to me January 22, 1978 when just before midnight, five minutes to be exact, doctors performed a cesarean section on my mother and pulled me out. Weighing in at 7 pounds 4 ounces, my dramatic entrance didn't stop there. I also was born with a congenital heart defect and a sixth finger on my right pinky. If these were indications of how I was to be later in life, it should have been known then that nothing about me would be normal. Granted there are other people born with these issues and yes some at the same time, however, the number is far fewer than what is considered normal births. Most times, surgery is needed for these birth defects but by the grace of God I would need none. My grandmother was a praying woman. And she used the precious God given gift of laying of hands on me and God healed my body. The hole in my heart closed on its own and my parents were spared the horrific experience of surgeries and back and forth visits to the hospital.

I was told that I was a feisty child. Always had an opinion, always in trouble, and could come up with a lie real quick if I thought it would keep me from getting in trouble. Maybe that is why at first I wanted to be an attorney when I grew up. As I write this even now I think, "aren't those the requirements for law enforcement?" I know not often does one remember a lot from early childhood and actually had it not been for the stories of relatives I would not even think the memories were mine. I can recall things that happened to me as early as two years old. I did not understand them, but I remember them. Maybe that was just the gift that God gave me. You know, I was supposed to remember. I know that there came a time in my life when I decided the generational curses in my family I wanted them to stop with me, I wanted to be used to bring an end to a lot of unspoken things families face, especially mine. I wonder if that is why He allowed me to retain the things that I do. Even now, my memory amazes those that know me. I know stuff like phone numbers after hearing them one time, credit card numbers with the CVC code, and the favorite drinks and likes of every preacher that has come to minister the word at the house of worship I attend, *TrueWay Apostolic Ministries.*

I was the first born child of five girls, whom you will meet later as we walk through the memories of my life, the first born grandchild on the maternal side of my family, and the third born grandchild on the paternal side. These things set me up real good to be one spoiled brat. I am sure I don't have to tell you that I milked it for all it was worth. I was spoiled and I know I was spoiled. I did not need to be told that I was, but I have heard it too. One of my big cousins that I liken to as a sister told me she could not stand me because I was so spoiled. We laugh about it now, but their efforts to get me whoopings were always in vain.

You know how there is that child in the family that does the most but if they cry the right way or just look a little sickly or something, the beat down was forgotten? Yea, I had some of those moments.

Funny what the brain will allow you to remember. I was just three years old when my paternal grandmother passed, but I remember getting away with things my older two cousins couldn't. It could have been because I was the baby, but one thing she didn't play was anybody messing with her grandkids and especially me. This wasn't always the case with the other side of my family. Granted we all come from some sort of dysfunction, if we will be honest, but my two families were like night and day. Speaking of, when you get to the maternal side, it was a blended family in itself because my maternal grandmother's family and my maternal grandfather's family were so close we just blended in as one big family. You ever went to a family reunion or wedding and heard the introductions of "this is your second cousin so and so or this is your aunt so and so"? Well in my family, aunts are really cousins and cousins are not really cousins depending on the distance of heritage.

What do I mean? Well if you are like a fourth or fifth cousin, "you don't count". The aunts that were cousins were just called aunt because it seemed the right thing to do because of the age difference. Can you believe some of them would even get mad if you didn't address them as such? Yea, crazy I know. I hope I didn't just lose you with that little breakdown, believe me, the whole one would really leave you saying, "WHAT??"

When I was four a bunch of my cousins and I were playing together which as you read this book, wasn't abnormal. We were together a lot, but one of the older ones decided that they wanted to teach us how to kiss. A couple of us got the short end of the stick and were the test dummies for them to experiment what they wanted to go and do with the boys. We were kissed and even slapped because we did not know to use our tongue. Yes, I was four. But when you put a bunch of kids together and the ages range from 4-12, you never know what you going to get in that group. The older ones are always trusted to watch the younger ones but in actuality, us younger ones use to watch the older ones. We saw them do a lot of things and some of those things were done to us.

I don't have much to share with you about the first five years of my life. I think it is a blur because I was having so much fun. Looking back over pictures from that time, I always had a smile on my face, my family was always doing something, and I had the hottest and newest toys of that time in my possession. One might say that I didn't need anything and that I had it made. I can remember people telling me that I should not have had any complaints and that I did not have any reasons to. I guess if you look at it from the perspective of I had loving parents who provided a roof over my head, food on the table, and clothes on my back I should not have.

But my childhood memories and that of my sisters changed as we got older. I know I am telling my story in this book and there will be times that I can't help but to bring one of them up, but we have some of the most amazing testimonies that I have ever heard a person tell. When God releases them to tell theirs, I can imagine what God will do in the younger ones behind me because of it.

My sister, Tiffany and I have the most memories of the five of us, but as we got older and started sharing secrets as sisters do we learned a lot and we took an oath amongst the five of us that some of those things ended with us. My sisters and I would have what was called "Sister Night", of course this came after Tiffany and I moved out, but we would get together with each other, and sometimes some cousins too, and just talk and party with each other all night long. I will mention these nights again later in this book.

Chapter Two
Christina's Childhood

When it was just Tiffany and I, keep in mind we were five years apart, most times I had her with me. Tiffany was like my baby as I had been everyone else's baby when I first got here. I could barely move without her. She hated to see me leave her. And even if we were with other kids, Tiffany still only wanted me. I was her safety net. My grandmother says that she remembers looking out the window once and she saw me walking in with a baby on one arm and a diaper bag on the other. My mom was coming in behind me, but she had different objects in her hands. Grandma says that she had a cigarette in one hand and a beer in the other. This to me was of no surprise because I remember all the parties and card games my parents use to have. And I remember Tiffany was like my baby. At first I treated her like a baby doll, just tossing her around, but eventually I grew to love her and knew I had to protect her. As you will see later in my life, I loved to party, but truth be told, the apple didn't fall too far from the party tree. My parents loved to party too, and when they partied, they partied hard.

I would never put them all out, but I put a couple of old pictures on my Facebook page a while ago from the old days as they are called. You hardly see any without the Budweiser cans littering the table and coffee tables in the background. I believe for a while, our house was the house to hold the card games. I never understood what was so fascinating about them until I had my own one day and learned that I made money off of every one else gambling. Do not take this as a plug to push card games now y'all. I am just telling you that I see why we had so many. Like I was saying, my cousins and I learned a lot from watching them when they did not think they were being watched. I know that goes with children period. I know we must be careful what we do around them, but during that time, it was not a real big concern. Although my parents ended up giving their lives to Christ and got us into the church, the memories of the past were still there and when I got grown enough and bad enough I would repeat a lot of their mistakes.

*****

I have a cousin who although younger than me (even though it was just a year), we use to always and when I say always get caught, I mean always, and we would get beat down for dry humping. It is not funny but I actually laughed at the memory of it when God told me to write about it. We never touched each other, although we did kiss on the lips, but we were like two little rabbits, just without the actual intercourse. I would always be on the bottom and he would be on top of me just hunching away.

We would get a whooping and separated for a while and then because we were family, we ended up back together doing it again. He was exposed to more than I was. I was told I knew better, because I was older, but he was the one that would tell me of the movies he had seen and the magazines he would look at when no one was looking. By this time in my life, I had already been kissed and touched so of course I did not argue with him when he wanted to sneak around the side of the house and play house with me. I would even tell him what the pictures meant because I had already been told and had heard some of the older relatives talking about it when they did not know I was listening. Even then, no one asked where those ideas came from. The solution was a switch. Well a switch did not help, nor did it deter me from experiencing it again.

An experience of going to my grandmother's house depended on two things, one the reason we were going and secondly on what mood my grandmother was in. She wasn't shy about telling my Mama about how she didn't want to watch them ugly tailed kids. We were the blackest and ugliest kids she had ever seen and she didn't want to be bothered. I know people say folks do not mean it when they say that, or my favorite is when someone tells me that is just how they person is, but when you a child, you don't understand sarcasm and those things hurt. When you are constantly told how ugly you are and it is even the source of an argument when someone tries to defend you and they get shut down, it stays with you for a long time. Tiffany tells the story of how she remembers being told she was the cutest ugly child one of our great aunts had ever seen. She had to stand in the middle of the floor while they decided if she was ugly or not and the conclusion was she was a cute ugly. You can imagine that this did nothing for our self-esteem.

For the longest time I would go to school and because I never thought I was pretty like the other girls, I would do other things to seek attention. I got in trouble in elementary school one time for asking this little boy to show me his penis. I think I was in the first grade. I may have been in the second. It was one of the many times that my parents separated and we were living at grandma's. But I do know I was too young to be seeking that kind of attention from a boy.

The punishment from that still stands out to this day. Not only did I get my tail whooped, but I had to watch my mother empty my piggy bank of all my money and put it in my sister Tiffany's bank. She said I did not deserve it. For a moment I hated Tiffany because of it, but one of my cousins helped me to realize it was not Tiffany fault. She did not ask for the money, so I stopped being mean to her when we went outside.

I have some really good memories of being at my grandmother's house too. If you are a part of a big family, you know the fun is never ending when you have what seems like a hundred cousins and you are set free in a yard the size of a football field. Oh the games and the trouble we got into. I am smiling now even as I type this to share with you. I had this one cousin who when we played kickball, he could kick the ball from here to Africa. Ok, I am exaggerating a little, but he could kick it really far. None of us kids ever liked it when he kicked the ball. We didn't want to be the ones to go get it for one and for two our rule was as long as the ball was out you could run around the bases as many times as you could before someone could get you out. Their team always won because of this rule, but it was still fun all the same.

Another memory from that yard is there was this sewage hole in the middle of the yard. To this day none of us understand why it was there, uncovered and we were sent out there on our own to play, but it never failed, although we knew it was there, at least one of us was going to slide through it and fall into the stinky gooey mess while the rest of us died and doubled over in laughter until it was our turn to fall victim to it.

One of my cousins was diagnosed as being a hemophiliac and he was not allowed to play with us because they were always afraid he was going to get hurt and bleed to death. We would sneak him outside when the older folks got so caught up in their gossip they did not notice him being missing. Or, if they gave him the freedom to come out, we would sneak him off the porch he was banished to, and let him jump on the trampoline with us or play basketball. Those were some of the most hilarious moments because we would get caught every time. One of my great aunts would always look out the window while he was in mid jump or had his foot up ready to run and she was start screaming bloody murder and he would be made to come inside. I can't tell you which look was more priceless, his smile from the fun he was having or the horror from the adults that would instantly check him for bumps and bruises. I know he appreciates us though to this day. We did not care about sickness or anything when it came to each other. We were family and all we wanted to do was have fun.

I miss those days despite the feeling of being unwanted that came with it. My sisters and I talk about it a lot. Linda, who is the middle child of the five of us, remembers lunch time the most. To know her now, you would understand why. The girl loves to eat. She takes pictures of her food before she eats and then she takes an after picture of what was left. Linda remembers beefaroni and orange Kool-Aid. She remembers getting our cups last and we always had the cup with the orange Kool-Aid residue in it. To this day she hates orange Kool-Aid. But we were fed and we ate till we couldn't eat anymore and that is all that matters right?

It is so weird though when I talk to some of my cousins and how all of us have the same memories of being there and being together but how differently we all were treated. Another reason I opted not to use names in this book is because of that. For one, it is not to stir up trouble and for two; they shouldn't be put on front street for just sharing. I wrote this after a vision God gave me, more than once may I add, of the healing that can take place through my story. I am writing it the way He told me to write it, as if I was talking to you the reader. It was very hard to watch when He began to reveal the things I am to share. It was even harder to write down.

Going back to memories. This memory I saw it, but didn't know that it was something that actually happened until my grandmother told the story one day. That is another thing, the childhood memory part of this book, every time I would ask God "did that really happen?" or "should I tell that story?" he would confirm it by sending someone to tell me the exact memory from my vision and how it happened.

I remember sitting in the car at this place that I later learned was the club, but I didn't know where we were at the time. My mother went in and told my cousins and me not to open the door for anybody. See she wanted to go out that night and at first my grandma wasn't going to keep us, but after she saw they were going to go anyway, she came and got us out the car. Although there are mean people everywhere, back then when you were around people that you knew, there wasn't too much of a worry of a serial killer snatching up your child. I do though feel that my mom probably knew deep down inside that my grandma would end up coming to get us anyway. Remember earlier I told you that they liked to party? Yea, by any means necessary. I think that is how I ended up being such a good dancer. I was at a lot of parties whosesoever they were held. When they were at grandma's house, they would be on the porch and the light bulb would be changed to blue or red. I would be in the house, but at some point, someone would come in and get me to dance some grown person down that thought they was out there killing it and my family would be like sit down. I would come out and Reebok and Cabbage Patch them right on up and after the crowd would crown me the winner I would be sent back in.

Chapter Three
Christina's Experiences

I am guessing that the first time I was touched inappropriately by a grown man I had already developed the reputation of being a child that just lies because when I talked about what had happened, it wasn't believed. I actually got smacked in the face for talking back to an adult and for calling an adult a liar, which is something you just did not do. My little sister Linda was born that year and my parents were on one of their many separations. We spent a lot of time in these housing projects in our area called Halifax Courts, which has since been torn down.

My cousins and I use to take my little sister Tiffany and our baby cousin outside to play and as long as we were back by the time the street lights came on, no one knew where we were or what we were doing. We went in the house to get water after a long day of playing and I went upstairs to see my new little sister for a second. I walked into the room and my mom had just finished kissing her then boyfriend and was getting ready to go get into the shower. There was always something about him that I didn't like and I use to hate it when they showed any kind of affection towards each other. Well, this particular time, when she went into the bathroom, I decided that I didn't want to him to watch my sister so I was going to wait around. My back was to the door when he came back in the room so by the time I felt his breath on my neck he was already too close. I turned around to ask him what did he want and he quieted me with a hard kiss right on my mouth. Keep in mind I am eight years old and of course I had never been kissed.

While he was yet kissing me, he was pulling me towards the door and he tapped it with his foot to close it just enough for privacy but not enough that we were closed in. He slipped his hand down my pants and grabbed me between my legs. The whole encounter couldn't have taken more than a minute, but it really felt like an eternity. I remember feeling like that it wasn't right what he was doing but at the same time, the tingly feeling that shot through my body made me want to feel it again. When the water turned off in the bathroom, he put his finger over his mouth in the shushing motion and sent me back down. I immediately went down and told my cousins what happened.

One of them informed me that he had done it to her before too, so at that moment we developed another secret among us kids that children just should not keep. As the days that went by, I use to try to make him want to touch me again. I was always in his face, I was always getting an attitude when he showed my mom too much attention, and I wanted him to make me feel that feeling again. Well, my actions didn't go unnoticed. My cousin's mom would tell my mother to send my mannish tail outside. That I was a fast little girl and she need to get me. This made me mad. But not at her. I was mad at him because he didn't even try to help defend me. Of course he didn't own up to what he was doing but he could have helped by taking some of the blame off me. Finally the straw that broke the camel's back came when I saw him hugging my cousin. It wasn't a hug of intimacy, but he was touching her never the less. I told how he had touched me and he didn't need to be hugging on her. He pleaded his innocence and it was my word against his. That hurt me a lot.

It hurt that I wasn't believed and it hurt me that he never touched me again. I hated him. I hated him so much and my cousins and I would plot his murder all the time. Well, as life would have it, we didn't have to kill him. He ended up dying a horrific death out of town. I remember we were at my grandmother's house when we got the news. My mama cried and I smiled. I smiled because in my mind at that time, that is what he deserved.

Usually when my grandma would go in on her rants about someone, I felt some type of way, but this day when she talked about him, I did not. I never knew until after he died that she did not like him anyway. She even said she did not like the way he looked at me. Who would of thought anyone noticed. Well he was gone by that time so all that was to me was noise, but I did feel like she kind of defended me that day. She was telling my mother to stop her moping and that was good enough for me.

So around this same time, they use to have what my cousins and I called "porn parties". Now keep in mind they were playing cards, drinking, smoking weed, and doing some of who knows what. Family and friends were deep in number and it was hard to tell who kin was and who wasn't from all the people that would be in the house. I know that my cousins and my little sister Tiffany would get sent to the back room to the cousin whose house it was room to play. We use to sneak out and make up reasons to leave the room so that we could either see what was going on or just so we could smell the sweet smelling smoke that filled the atmosphere. We didn't know at the time we were getting contacts but we knew it made us really giggly and hungry so it was all good.

In the beginning of the party every time we opened the door, it would be noticed and some responsible adult would scream out *"which one of yall is that? Get back in that room"*. We would laugh and run back in the room for fear of catching the wrath of someone that didn't mind beating a kid down for seeing them do their dirt. Anyway, the later it would get, the more intoxicated everyone was, the least they noticed us coming out the room. We would sneak into the living and see the naked men and women doing all sorts of things on the television screen and then we would go into the room and "practice" with each other. But there were times when going to the bathroom you would run into some drunk who just didn't understand why they couldn't go in the bathroom with you. We would be told by men who were peeing just pee in the bathtub because two of us can fit in here. And because they were "family" we didn't see anything wrong with it. We never talked about it because for one it was exciting to us to be there and two we had long discovered the golden rule of staying in a child's place.

Chapter Four
Christina's Parents

Around 1988 my parents were back together again and we moved to a neighborhood on the outskirts of Garner, North Carolina called Camelot. I received another sister that year, Veronica, and I just remember her being this little chinky eyed thing that just laid there and slept all the time.

By this time, I was starting to find a little piece of my inner cuteness, but not for the right reason. I know now, it was an unclean spirit that was the source, but I was attracting older men. To someone that felt ugly most of their life, this was an exciting thing. I was ten years old and attending Garner Elementary School. I struggled with myself image a lot because we lived in a predominately white neighborhood and naturally I stood out but I wanted to fit in so bad.

I remember when my mother finally let me go to a sleepover at the neighbor's house that stayed behind us. I was the only black child there and we stayed up all night long. Literally, no sleep from the time we got there til the time the sun came up. What I remember about that night is the torture I went through from my so called friends. They reminded me that I was different and they hesitate to make sure that I didn't forget that I was black. I could of easily went home, but I wanted to be a part of something so bad, I laughed at all the racist jokes and pretended I was having just a good time as they were. If only I had been taught what myself worth was at that time, I know that night would have been differently. The next morning it was someone's bright idea to go walking around the neighborhood. It's like seven in the morning and we just going to go for a stroll.

My mom worked at night and I knew that she would be coming home but I had hoped she wouldn't run into us. While we were walking, we find out one of the girls had stolen her mother's cigarettes and we were going to all try one. As luck would have it, just as soon as I light mine up and pull into the neighborhood who should pull in? Yep, you guessed it, my Mama. I laugh now as I remember how I turned my head and looked the other way and tried to pretend that not only could I not see her but that she couldn't see me either. Yes, you read that correctly, I convinced myself if I didn't look she wouldn't know it was me, but I was the only black child in the group and what mother doesn't know what her child looks like. She didn't get me right then. I immediately knew my consequence was going to be even worse because my mom cared nothing about embarrassing me and because she didn't stop, I knew she was going to get me for real. So we made it back to my friend's house and everyone decided that we were going to go to sleep.

By His Stripes

Well, it was like my mom had radar or something because as soon as I lay down she called for me to come home. I was so tired and I just wanted to take a nap, after all, I had stayed up all night long. When I walked in the door she didn't beat me at first. The list of chores she gave me was beating enough. Don't get me wrong, I did get it, but the lack of sleep and excessive cleaning was punishment without it.

While living in this same house, I had another experience with someone older touching me and making me feel like I was older than I was. The guy next door, my friends and I secretly called him "Chester Chester Child Molester". You would think with a nickname like this, I would have stayed away from him, but I didn't. They had a trampoline and I used to go over and jump on it. The kid in me loved the trampoline but what I felt was lack of attention in my life had me loving how he looked at me.

See, my family wasn't and still isn't that big on saying I love you just because. I was never told by my dad that I was pretty. My mother did give us the don't let nobody touch you in your private areas rule but honestly we all thought it was just another rule to follow. So when my neighbor started noticing me, it was once again exciting like a couple of years prior when I was touched by a grown man who should of known better. I still have the scar on my shoulder from the beat down my mom gave me when she caught me over the neighbor's house. It wasn't even just the fact that I was over there but I was inside, and I was inside alone with him. What they don't know is what happened. I was jumping on the trampoline with the little girl that lived next door and her brother was watching us from the back porch. At the time I think he was around twenty years old. I can still see his face and remember that he looked a lot like Johnny Depp's character on Twenty-One Jump Street. I had to use the bathroom and at his suggestion to go in the house instead of going home, which was right next door, I went in. When I came out he was waiting for me in the kitchen and offered me something to drink. After I finished, instead of going back out, I lingered a little bit hoping he would keep talking to me. He didn't keep talking, but he did show what his interest was. He too grabbed me as I had previously received and kissed me. My heart was beating so fast as I was waiting on what I knew was to come next. That touch that brought the tingly feeling always came after the kiss. He did it and the feeling that I had waited years to feel came rushing back between my innocent legs.

As I was leaving the house feeling like a big girl, who should catch me coming out? You guessed it, my mother. She didn't ask any questions, she sent me right into to remove my clothes while she went to the back yard and grabbed a handful of switches. She didn't ask what happened, she didn't ask why I was in there and I didn't tell her. I took my beating. All she knew was I was coming out of a house I shouldn't have been in. Somewhere between the skin being completely peeled off my shoulder and feeling like I was going to have an asthma attack, I felt like shouting at her to go jump on "Chester" for kissing me, but I didn't. I honestly didn't see what good it would have done. I know that her biggest fear was me being grown and not acting my age, but honestly at that time, my being punished everytime something like that came up only made me feel like it was something wrong with me and that was why things like that kept happening. If I had any control over it, I do feel like I would of stopped it. I think parents took the spare the rod scripture a little too literal then. Also, the generation before me was not taught how to sit down and just talk to their kids.

Chapter Five
Christina's Hurts

December 1, 1991 at 5:32pm on a Sunday evening is a day I will always remember. I was thirteen years old and it was the day that I lost my virginity. I had already tried once and it didn't work. Both of the guys were members of the holiness church I went to when I was younger and we had services all day long every Sunday. We used to huddle together in Sunday School class and try to figure out who we were going to go home with after the first service since we knew we would be returning that evening anyway.

I remember looking up to some of the older girls in the church and wanting to be just like them. The church I attended was a fairly large one and the cliques had their sections of the church throughout the building. The teens had the back of the church on lock. One of the topics that we discussed was sex. Now that I think about it, it should have been the lack thereof of sex. The ones that I thought was doing it weren't. I found this out through a very hard and embarrassing lesson.

My first attempt didn't go so well and honestly the setting was much more appropriate than the setting that I ended up losing my virginity in. The first attempt was at the home of one of the church members but the guy was what I now know is impotence, that day. Now flash forward a couple of months. So there was this guy whose family had always been a part of the church family but they had been living out of town. When his family moved back, he was the one that all the girls were falling all over, me included. The first time he paid me a piece of attention I thought it was the greatest thing since slice bread. I was so excited every time we ran into each other in the halls of the church with no one around which was rare. One day we planned to meet in one of the unlocked Sunday School classrooms to talk about our "relationship". First of all, it wasn't a relationship, it was him recognizing that I was desperately seeking attention and plus he had already thought I was open because I talked like I had the experience. So we met and kissed and decided that the next week we would leave during the second service and basically we planned to have sex.

Because our church was so radical and the shouting could go on for hours once it got started, we decided no one would miss us and I would meet him out front and we would leave for rendezvous. I went and hoped in the passenger side of his daddy's Cadillac and we set off looking for a close place to go park so we wouldn't be gone too long. We ended up at the local middle school parking lot beside the dumpster. When he parked the car he got in the back seat and motioned for me to join him. At this point my heart started beating fast because I realized it was going to happen for real this time. I had already learned and mastered what an erection looked like. Sitting beside him I suddenly remembered that I was a little girl and I got nervous. I was so nervous that his lame attempt to calm me down actually worked. He told me that if I sucked it first, it wouldn't hurt as much. Well, he lied. It was the most painful experience I ever had. I bled really bad. I bled all on him and some on the seat. He got angry and was more so concerned with his father's car seats than the fact that I was bleeding. So between the pain and the blood, I had to hurry up and clean up so we could get back to the church. The five minute drive felt like hours as he dropped me off right before the church so no one could see me getting out the car. As I pushed through the pain between my legs, I went to the bathroom to stuff paper towels in my underwear. When I came out, I felt like the whole back section of the church knew. I didn't care because I had become one of the girls, or so I thought. I remember when I told one of them what happened, she got mad at me. She told me I was lying on him and she said I also lied about it being my first time. She then went and pulled him to the side and he told her his version and that was the story that was believed. Within a week he made one of my friend's his girlfriend and I was extremely crushed and very jealous.

During that time, I had what was called a PARTNER. PARTNER was a program kind of like Big Brother/Big Sister and mine came to get me the next night. I told her all about what happened and she took me to Planned Parenthood to get on birth control. I promised to pay her back when I could. Keep in mind, at this time I am thirteen years old. I did not have a job nor did I have a way to get one. By that January she had gotten tired of waiting and she came to my house not too long after my fourteenth birthday and requested her money back from my Mom. Well, the secret was out. My mother got on the phone and called my dad and told him how I had been trying to have sex. I did not dare say it to her, but I was thinking to myself I did not try, I did have sex. I got a whooping of course. (Yes, a month later). The speech I got was the quickest way to hell was by having sex and I didn't have any business doing it.

    Not too long after this, my uncle came to live with us. What we didn't know at the time was he was living with the virus that causes AIDS known as HIV. My sister Tiffany and I shared a room, but when he came to stay we had to give it up for him to have. We didn't understand so naturally we resented him a little bit because of it. We had what we called the "glass house" but in actuality it was a sun room that was a bonus to our house. We as kids were not allowed to go in there, but my uncle got to lie in there all day every day. He also got to choose what we ate for dinner and for the longest time it was Little Caesar's Pizza with real tomatoes on it. I laugh now thinking about it because what kid wouldn't want to eat pizza every day, but we didn't. So before we knew he was sick, we catered to him and got beat down if we didn't. I think it would have been a better a transition if our mom had just told us what was going on, but my uncle had already been shunned by a lot of the family and I guess she was protecting him from us by not telling us the truth. As you can see, my family wasn't big on communicating. I do wish she had told us though. Needless to say, his old boss ended up building a room on to my grandmother's house just for him and he was able to go back home for the last few months of his life. I found out what was wrong with him from one of my cousins who thought we knew and she asked my sister and I how it felt to have him living with us.

When he passed, it was a very painful time. I think they knew it was going to be soon because a lot of them were there when it happened. My sisters and I were at home. I was watching them and talking on the phone when I got a beep. I remember clicking over and hearing these piercing screams in the background and before a word was said I knew. I knew he was gone. I cried so hard. I cried for the lost and I cried because I was so glad we had made up for how I acted when he stayed with us. He died in Christ and that was awesome in itself. My friend stayed on the phone with me just comforting me. She really didn't know what to say, but she stayed on the phone and just let me cry. I didn't want my sisters to see my tears so I stayed in my parent's room until I got it all out.

His funeral was also a memorable moment of his death. My sister and I were not allowed to ride with the family to the church. We had to ride with a family friend that we called

Auntie. It was so unfair that we went through so much with him and we were sat at the back of the church for his home going like we weren't even a part of the family. When the family came in we felt like outsiders watching all of our cousins and aunts and uncles come in and receive condolences from the visitors. That hurt in itself because that was our uncle. We were hurting too, but our pain was not recognized. It took a while for me to get over that. I held that grudge for the longest time. But we were used to getting the short end of the stick like that. That was just the way the cookie crumbled for us.

Chapter Six
CHRISTINA'S NEW ADVENTURE

As much as I was seeking attention when I got to high school, and as much as I wanted to be like the good girls, I did not recognize it when I had the chance to. I remember there was a rapper out by the name of Boss. I have no idea what to tell you she rapped, but I just remember her. She wore red lipstick, a bandana on her hair, and baggy jeans. I started immolating my style of dress after her. I thought I was her actually, with the exception of the fact that I could not rap of course.

Again, during one of the times I had run away from home, I remember going to stay with a so called friend. I had tried to catch a cab to her house and the meter got to the amount of money I had and I told the cab driver to just let me walk the rest of the way. He had not problem letting me out seeing as how we were at this point well outside the city limits. While walking to her house the sun began to go down and it got extremely dark. Now by car, it would of taken approximately five minutes to get there, but walking at night uphill with no street lights, you can imagine that my troop was dragging on what felt like forever. This guy on a red truck pulled up and asked me where I was headed. Keep in mind I got on my "Boss gear" so I am feeling real thug like and just safe. I told him up the road to the house across from the stop sign and he told me to get in. It would be two hours before I made it to her house.

I am shaking my head at how naïve I was. I figured nothing really could happen since we were right down the road from her house. I mean, it was in walking distance, which is what I was doing right? Well I was wrong. I am so blessed that what happened was the worse of it. He could of killed me. I got to her house just for her mother's boyfriend to say I could not stay that night. I broke down. I had just endured the most horrific two hours of my life and all for him to say I could not stay. I went through a lot to get there and I was broke and I ended up in the backseat of their car headed back home.

You know, I learned from my own life to validate my daughters. I know my parents loved me. I have no doubt at all that they cared deeply for me and wanted the best for my sisters and I, but they never said it. Telling them that we loved them made them feel weird obviously based on the responses we would get. We would have to keep saying it before we got a love you too. Sometimes they would say just an "mmmh hmmmm" and that was it. We hated it, but again, what could we do about it.

I remember the first time I knew my uncle looked at me as more than a niece. I was extremely young, and I thought it was something I did. I never considered the fact that he just had a problem. It was just something about how he looked at me, you know how there is something in someone's eyes that just says more than what should be said. My sister Tiffany said he made her feel creepy because he always needed help with stuff that didn't need to be helped. She was never touched by him, but before she understood what the gift of discernment was, she knew something just wasn't right about it. She use to complain about having to be around him and she would get in trouble for being grown, notice a trend here? So to protect her from the things that I knew interested him, I would make sure to keep his attention whenever he was around.

Up until him, I had only been touched and kissed and had never felt another man's penis. He was the first one I felt and saw. Being young it was scary and it appeared to have its own large life but he would only make me touch it. When he kissed me, he would ask me to kiss him again because my lips were so soft. "Give me another one", he would say. It really got old after a while but it did not stop. He liked for my small hands to rub it and it excited him to see the curiosity in my face as to how it would be asleep and wake up. I didn't know about erections then so I thought this was something magical.

For years this went on just touching and rubbing on both of our parts. What I didn't get and still don't get is how no one saw the looks that he gave me. How no one noticed the difference when he came around. But as I said, for years, it went unnoticed. This too became a secret that my sister, my cousins, and I shared that just should have been told. We did end up having sex once. It only happened once and I was so sick after. I think that is why he did not try to have sex with me again. One of the many times I had ran away from home, I was hungry. I called him and asked him if he could feed me. He found out where I was and came and picked me up. The thing that is even more sickening is he talked to me about going back home. He told me that my parents loved me and they wanted the best for me.

While he was talking to me he was looking at me with that look that he had been looking at me with since I was younger. I remember rolling my eyes at him and asking him what would it take for him to stop looking at me like that. I asked him if he would just take me to get something to eat and drop me off where he got me from. He promised more if I would just lay with him one time. At that point I was desperate. I told him okay, that I would but he had to give me some money first. Before anything even happened I got scared. I remember saying no, this is not right and if you going to help me you should do it without me having to do this. He told me how much he loved me and reminded me of how he was the one to make me feel pretty when others made me feel ugly. He asked me if he had ever hurt me before and at that time my answer was no. I mean, he had not technically hurt me. I trembled and cried the entire time praying for it to end soon. There is no way to describe the level of disgust I felt. The worse part of it all was I had no way of washing him off of me for at least half the day after it happened. I went into a shell for a few weeks. I did not smile, I just did not care.

Again, I had convinced myself that this was all I was worth. I did not place any of the blame on him. I did not acknowledged the fact that he was the one that should of known better. I did not think about when he asked if he had ever hurt me not only had he, but by asking me to give him my body he was doing it at that moment. It was during one of vulnerable states that I was to place myself in. I was sixteen years old. A lot of people would say that I was old enough to know better. But the thing with sexual abuse is more than just knowing better. Although I had a child, I still had yet to learn myself worth. And the attention of men was the icing on the cake for me being a girl who never felt pretty enough. You will hear more of this later. I have to back track for a minute or two to get you here.

I know this book is a flashback in itself, but I have to go back to when I was fourteen. I forgot to tell another story that plays a part in the story. Wonder how many of you reading this has a memory of stealing your parent's car. I stole my mother's hooptie when she was asleep and thought I could quickly drive it around the corner while she was sleeping without getting caught. As I was sneaking out, my sisters begged to go and seeing as how I didn't want them to wake her up while I was gone, I decided to take them with me. Now keep in mind, I was not going to leave the neighborhood. As we were going up the street, I guess I ended up on the wrong side of the road because I almost ran into another car head on. This did not deter me nor make me want to turn around. I knew that I may as well finish the ride since I was already out. What I didn't know was that the person I almost hit knew not only my mom's car, but knew my family. While we were riding still the phone call was going forth to my grandmother's house. No sooner than we pulled up at the house and got in good, my secret was out. Here comes my family waking my mom up and telling her what I had done. After I got beat down, it was decided that something was terribly wrong with me and I needed help. This stunt just earned me a visit and stay at the local mental health hospital, Holly Hill.

During my stay at Holly Hill I met a lot of interesting people. Even now as I type this, I am laughing because how can one say they met interesting people at a mental hospital. What other kind of people are there to meet? While there, the sexual demon that had been living in me was awakened when I met this guy that I thought was the most beautiful thing I had ever seen. Never mind my location and there was something wrong with these people, I decided I wanted him and I knew once we made eye contact that he wanted me too. We started spending our off time together in the recreation room. Keep in mind there was no privacy, but we spent as much time as we could talk and getting to know each other. I learned that he lived in Holly Springs, NC which wasn't too far from where I was living at the time, which was Cary, NC. We decided when we got out we would hook up, no matter how long it took.

I instantly went on my best behavior so I could not only earn privileges but so I could be released soon with a clear mind bill of health. I aced the entire ink blot test. My roommate told me what they wanted to hear when I went to my counseling sessions seeing as how she had been in there a couple of times, she knew all too well.

When I went home I started accepting his phone calls and talking to him while he was completing his stay there. I couldn't wait for who I considered my boyfriend to come home. I really thought I was in love and the lustful awakening that had been ignited when I was in there had to be fed.

Those of you reading that grew up in holiness churches, I am sure you have heard the saying that the Holy Ghost will tell on you. Well, the statement is more than true which you will see more and more as you read my story. When he got out he found a job and got a car and his next stop was to see me.

I was so happy and waiting for my father to fall asleep so that I could sneak him into our garage. My mom worked at night and I wouldn't of dared tried it if she was home because that woman never slept. We would have been caught for sure. I know we were caught anyway, but I just wouldn't have tried it with her. I really didn't think my dad paid us that much attention so I just knew that it would be easier to get away with him. So he comes over and we are in the garage doing what we were doing when my dad got up. It's like he knew, he got up and came straight to the garage. We didn't have light on but he knew. I tried to hold the door so he couldn't open it while my boyfriend sat on the couch stuck and scared with no nerves to run when my dad overpowered me and snatched the door open.

The look is in eyes was far from anger. It was hurt. He was so hurt and so disappointed and that would have been punishment enough for me, but of course it didn't end there. I will never forget that day as long as I live, but it did nothing for the strong sexual spirit that I had yet to be delivered from. My beat down and having to know that the whole family was talking about me did nothing to make me not want to do it again. I just had to figure out how not to get caught next time.

Later that school year I was in a play at school. It was the Diary of Anne Frank. I was so excited about my part in the play. I was the narrator. Yes, the narrator. But to me that was just as important as any other part. I set the tone for the play. Without me, you would not know what was going to happen or why. As narrator I was guaranteed to be in the whole play versus just a scene or two. Although I was wanted to act because it had yet to be seen that I really was and still is a good actress, just being there was enough for me. We all got dressed up and made up for our parts. At the dress rehearsal we practiced in our full get ups and when I went home I was blasted by my dad for wearing make-up. He was livid. He made me wash my face and told me that I was going to hell if I did it again. See at the time, the church we attended, you weren't allowed to wear make-up or jewelry. Women were even forbidden to wear pants in the sanctuary so me coming home with make-up was a big thing. My dad did not care that it was for a play. He just saw the mess as he called it on my face and he strongly forbidden me from wearing it again. Well, I didn't listen. The next night when we were getting dressed for the actual performance, I didn't want to be left out. I let them make me up again. My mom took us to my dad's job after the play was over and how the performance went did not matter. All he saw was my face and that was the end of that. I was in so much trouble. That was the last school play I was in too.

There were Christmas plays at our church, but we were never a part of them. Tiffany still to this day is asking God to help her get over the fact that we were never asked to be a part of them and we always wanted to so bad. Our grandfather's wife was in charge of the Drama Department and by the time all the parts were given out to the big names in the church and all of her nieces and nephews, there wasn't anything for us to do anyway. I will never forget when I finally got my big break to act at the church. It was during one of the yearly Black History Month programs and I wanted to be in it and begged. Every Sunday in Sunday School I worked on my part unbeknownst to a lot of people. When it was time, I dressed the part of a slave and went out and nailed the part of Sojourner Truth. I will never forget the responses when I gave the performance of a lifetime citing "Ain't I A Woman" by heart. It felt so good to be recognized for something good for a change and it felt even better for it to be known I was good for something after all.

My parents say I never got to do anything because I didn't know how to act, but I acted the way I did because I never got to do anything. It was a no win situation and again, had there been communication, I think that would have been established a long time before some of the situations I was in got out of hand.

Chapter Seven
Christina Moves .... Again

By the time I got to the ninth grade, we were preparing to move to Raleigh, North Carolina. I don't know why we were moving, I was just glad that I had stayed at a middle school the whole three years. I had went to five different elementary schools because of us moving a lot and my parents constantly separating but getting back together and for a while I had got tired of having to make new friends, although that was not very hard for me to do.

So anyway, two weeks after I started high school, we moved. Before we left, my mother was told that I was going to end up pregnant and that I would probably have five or six kids all with different fathers. I didn't learn this until later so you can imagine that it didn't help that within a year of us moving, I did end up pregnant. When I first got to my new high school, I could immediately tell it was going to be a different experience from the country schools I was used to. There was so much freedom, although as an underclassmen, I should not have had half the privileges that I did. I became well known around the school and my lovable con artist personality made it easy for me to get notes to go to the office for no reason other than I just didn't want to be in class at the time. I became extremely close to the

Attendance Office Manager and this was my golden ticket to roam the halls as I pleased.

Being the new girl, I was immediately noticed and by this time I knew that I had a big butt and a cute smile so I would sneak the clothes I wanted to wear under the clothes I left the house in. My favorite cousin was a few years older than me and I would get stuff from her that was very form fitting and sexy and wear it to turn heads as I walked the halls. I didn't know that I didn't have to dress like that to get attention. I didn't know that the guys that I really wanted to notice me didn't want the girls dressed the way I was. I thought that was what I had to do to get the attention and keep the attention that was coming my way.

Now this is the part of my life where the sexual demon that was in me was really precedent in my life. I was even trying to seduce my teachers during this time which it worked in the sense of them letting me miss class but still passing me. Not all of them were under my spell though, but enough for me to think that I wasn't in danger of failing. I just wasn't concerned at the time. The sad part though, I am and was a highly intelligent person. I could miss a week of class, read the lessons in a night and then go in and ace the test. It only took me one time of looking to learn something. I just didn't care. I had been introduced to a whole new world. I learned how to drive, skip school, ride the city bus, and forge signatures on my hall passes. I thought I had it going on.

One of the most memorable moments my mother truly knew best was when I was dating this guy that I just could not see was no good for me. She used to let him come over and visit, but she was not having it with me going off anywhere with him. He and I were really good friends I thought, and of course in my eyes he could do no wrong. He was not the popular type, he was actually very quiet, at least when he was around me. We could talk for hours on end about absolutely nothing and I remember how I thought he had the most beautiful smile known to man. Although I was young, I felt like I knew everything and I just could not understand why although my mom tolerated him, she really did not like him. She was not mean to him, outside of her normal self, but it was cool. The only part that had me throwing tantrums was not being able to even walk with him to the park and definitely not get in the car and go with him anywhere.

There was this one particular day he came over more agitated than normal. He would not tell me what was bothering him. He would just pace and mumble as I stared at him trying to figure out what was wrong. I had never seen him smoke before and he asked me to go across the street to my cousin house to see if he had a cigarette. That should have been the first clue that he was not in his normal state of mind, but I still did not put the clues together.

He begged me to ask my mom if she would let me ride with him to the store. He promised he would bring me right back and he just wanted me to be by his side for a moment. My mother worked third shift and I was not going to wake her up to ask her to answer a question I already knew the answer to. I went in the house long enough to pretend that I asked and came to let him know that she had said no. He left and that was the last time I saw him in person again.

When he did not call me that night, I was naturally upset and could not figure out why. I called his parents house repeatedly to just be told he was not home yet. Later that night my phone calls went unanswered until it was too late to call and I had to wait until the next day.

He did not meet me behind the school gym as he usually did and I really started wondering why. I thought he had broken up with me because I could never do anything. Thoughts of him with his new girlfriend tortured me the rest of the day.

My mom would watch the soap opera Young and the Restless and it was during this show that a breaking news bulletin came up announcing a robbery and fatal shooting at a small country store that I learned what happened to my boyfriend. The description and police sketch of the man the police were looking for looked just like my boyfriend. The store was not even five minutes from where we were living but I still refused to believe it was him. I asked my mother if she thought it looked like him and she said a little bit but my doubt made her hesitate because if anyone would know, it should have been me right?

It wasn't long before we learned it was him and not only was it him, his own parents were the ones that turned him in. I can not imagine what they went through as parents having to make this decision, but I looked at my mom like a hero that day. If she was not so hard on me and let me do what I wanted to do, I would have been with him when he committed that crime and there is not telling how the story would of ended. I know either way, it would not be pretty.

I intended on writing him a letter, but it was not long before he left my attention span. What is the old saying? Out of sight out of mind? Well it is true. As in love with him as I was, I quickly moved on to the next person that showed me a little attention and was in love all over again.

Right around this time is when I started running away from home. I just wasn't happy. Don't get me wrong, life wasn't horrible. We went on family trips and stuff. But our activities revolved around each other as siblings. We had a living room we couldn't sit in because all of my dad's glass pieces were set up all around it which limited us to our bedrooms and the dining room/den area. Tiffany and I were responsible for making sure we cooked and cleaned and watched out for the others because Mama worked at night and slept in the day and daddy worked during the day and needed his sleep at night.

Sometimes it just got irritating always having to make sure they were straight before we could do anything. There was a store in our neighborhood that was actually in walking distance from our house. Tiffany's best friend came to get her to ride to the store and before she could go she had to clean the whole house. Mind you the store was right up the street, but it didn't matter. I just didn't want to be there. The first time I ran away came after my mother found my diary that I didn't want her to read. I felt like it was my own personal get away and it was the only thing I had for myself. I tried my best not to let her read it.

We played tug a war over that journal for a few minutes before she reminded me that she was the mother and I was the child. I just remember looking up with her sitting on my chest and one hand around my neck with the other hand on the phone telling whoever was on the other line to come get me before she killed me. To this day she still doesn't know who she called, but it just so happened that one of my aunts was coming by and she stopped by that day and got there in time to get her off of me. That wasn't anything but grace and favor on both of our lives that day because it could have ended so much worse.

I waited until she went to work and ran away from home. I had met this girl and her mom was never really home so I went to her house. She was younger than me but this girl was so sexually advanced you would have thought she was older than she was. She and her cousins had me some of everywhere the few days I was with them. There was a local nightclub in the area called Kami Kaze and at the young ages of fourteen and fifteen we were up in there. I want to say the age requirement was twenty one and over, but because of who we knew and how we dressed it didn't matter. So it was then that I was introduced to marijuana and alcohol. I was having what I thought was the time of my life until we both became runaways together and the police was sent to the house we were at. It was then I learned her real age. Well, she went home and the police took me to the doctor and took me home too. Later I learned that I had contracted chlamydia. The disease itself is not even the worse part of the experience. When my mom found out, she wouldn't let me go to the bathroom and close the door. She didn't want me to sit on her toilet. She hardly wanted me to use her tissue. For a few days this lasted before I ran away again. Honestly, I was so ticked off at how she was treating me behind chlamydia but I remembered just a few years before my uncle lived with us with AIDS and he was treated like a king. That truly hurt me.

This time when I ran away, I did not have a set destination to go to. I stayed with whoever had a bed I could sleep in. Many times sharing that bed meant sharing my body, but just so I didn't have to go home, I paid that price. There were so many nights that I almost called and said please come get me, but I would think of the consequences of what I would suffer and just chose to stay on the streets. It wasn't until I was raped at knife point that I realized I needed to go home. I had been sleeping in this guy's basement for a few days. Every now and then he would bring me food to eat and we would have sex. But then he would have to sneak back off upstairs as not to give it away to anybody that he had something going on downstairs. For hours at a time I would stay down there quiet and bored with nowhere to go and nothing to do.

One night he came running down and told me I had to go because he had family coming over and they would be coming downstairs. I didn't know what that had to do with me but he reminded me that I couldn't get caught there. So in the middle of the night, I had to leave. While wondering the streets trying to figure out where to go, this guy approached me and offered me his jacket. He asked me if I would like to come to his house for the night. At first I was like no thank you. He convinced me by saying that his sister and his nieces were there and that I didn't have to worry. Naturally that sounded safe to me and besides, it was so cold out there that he didn't have to argue with me much longer anyway. So I went. When we got there, I guess he went to the back to let them know he had company and that we would be in the front. He got me some blankets and a pillow and I proceeded to lie on the floor. Well, he ended up coming to lie beside me, supposedly just to talk. I dozed off in the middle of his conversation which I guess made him mad because when I woke back up he had a knife to my throat and the point was sharp enough that it had pricked my skin and blood was running down my neck.

As he was unfastening his pants he told me if I screamed the sound would be cut off by the knife going in and cutting my voice box off. Seeing as how he already had the knife on me, I knew he would do it, even with his family in the house. After he had his way with me, I went to sleep only to be told what felt like minutes later it was time for me to go. Once again it was time for me to walk the streets like the zombie that I was because I just didn't want to go home.

Chapter Eight
Christina's Pain

Going back home again and returning back to school, there was a senior that I had caught the eye of. He was a good guy. He really started off as my best friend and it developed into more. We use to talk for hours and he was the first guy that actually started talking to me and at me. I didn't understand nor respect the quality of man that he was at the time, but looking back, I know that he was the type whose attention I really wanted. The first time we had sex I got pregnant. We cried together. I was fifteen years old. Before I had the chance to tell my family my mother told me. I still do not know how she found out. I just remember her being on the phone with someone and telling them how my daddy didn't believe in abortions so I was going to have to have the baby. She never hesitated to remind me that I was pregnant as if I was going to forget. But our relationship did not change at all because of it.

As my baby was growing in my stomach, I was forbidden to use a lot of things that she brought. Seeing as how I thought I was grown, I could take care of myself she would say. But my child's father was more than supportive. When I couldn't iron my clothes, he brought me my own iron and I would hide it until I needed it. The kitchen was cut off to me after certain hours and being pregnant, I had all kinds of crazy cravings at weird hours of the night. He use to buy me food and put it in the mailbox. I remember Hardee's had just come out with their Frisco Burgers and he would put me one in the box every night just about. He also worked at a grocery store so I had all the Twinkies, Strawberries, and Thousand Grand candy bars I could eat. I would share with my sisters but I had to be careful not to eat too much in the open because I would be accused of keeping stuff from them when truth was I was just trying to make it last. On my sixteenth birthday I remember sitting on the couch watching something on television and she came up to me and told me that if I hadn't been pregnant I could have been at the club right then with my cousins celebrating my birthday. When she turned her back I just rolled my eyes. This was not what I wanted to hear at that time. Needless to say the closer I got to my due date, the more excited she started getting about the fact that her first grandchild was coming.

When I went into labor she was the one that got me to the hospital and she was the one that kept the doctors in check. I will never forget her videoing the whole birth and how she had the camera zoomed in on areas I would of rather she didn't, but I am glad that she documented the experience. I am just glad that she was there period. My son's father was in the room too, but halfway through the birthing process he got sick and had to vomit so he left the room for a while. I would have been alone with doctors had it not been for my mom. Him getting sick was the funniest thing to her, so although she was laughing her butt off, just having her in there was very comforting.

By the time my son was a few weeks old, I had once again grown tired of the home life. I was now a mother to my own child but I was also still taking care of my little sisters as if they were my own. Not too long after he was born my sister Kayla developed an ear infection. Kayla was around three years old at the time. With my mom working at night and my dad sleeping, since I was already up with a new born, it was also my responsibility to take care of her too. That first night it seemed like when one finished crying and fell asleep, the other one would wake up. It was one of the most emotionally exhausting nights of my life. I cried with them. Each time a child would wake up crying I would comfort them and then I would cry myself.

It wasn't long after he was born that I returned to school and with all my absences and the fights that I had gotten into, it was decided that I needed to go to an alternative school. My education there was on and off again seeing as how that runaway spirit reared its head around the time my son was six months old. This time I ran a few counties away to my cousin house in Goldsboro, NC. Although she kind of let me have my own mindset with what I had going on, one rule she had was I had to go to school. So I enrolled in the high school and immediately was on the Most Hated List from the first day I walked through the halls. At this point there was no shame whatsoever in my game.

I was highly opinionated and didn't care about consequences. The guy my cousin was dating at the time had some sisters who instantly adopted me as one of their own. I just had that you either love me or hate me thing going on and luckily for me they loved me and to this day we still have a relationship. I didn't help the fire that was burning against me at the High School. I would add fuel to the fire every chance that I got. Once there was this girl talking to her boyfriend who I knew like me and while they were in mid conversation I went and took his hat right off his head.

See, someone like me needed her tail whooped, but someone who did the things that I did with no back up clearly had to be crazy. Once again being the new girl walking the halls, that sexual demon within me was awakened and thrived in the atmosphere of plenty. There was a local club called the Big Apple and one of my adopted sisters as I call them and I use to make it our business to go every chance we could. I remember the night Mobb Deep came to town and I called the club and promised we would work the door and whatever just so we could get in for free. She was infatuated with them and because she was my sis, I had to get us in there. That happened a lot, we clubbed knowing we should have been home, but shoot they let us in so we walked through the open door. But sometimes she didn't go and I just didn't want to stay home. It was on the nights that she didn't go that I got into the most trouble. Somehow I would always end up with a cup that I didn't ask for and it would end up with me waking up the next morning in a house I didn't know beside a man I had never seen. There was this one particular night that she didn't go out with me and I just had to go.

At the gas station I ran into a classmate that night and we both discovered we were heading to the same place. We had never really talked at school but we were in Gospel Choir together so I knew who she was. What's eerie is we sort of resembled each other but never really noticed it. That night I met these guys and usually I didn't care about leaving the club for an after party with whoever, but something wouldn't let me. I went and told my classmate bye, not because we were together but just because she was a familiar face and I left. She was talking to one of the guys that I had declined a date with. I didn't think nothing of it, honestly I don't remember his name nor what he looks like.

The next morning they found her body behind the club. It could have been me. But God blocked it that night for me. I felt so bad for her family but most of all I felt bad for her. She was just trying to have a good time and lost her life doing the very thing I had been doing. During this time I was dipping and dodging my family in Wake County. That was a very stressful time for them because description wise, they thought it was me and then add the fact that they hadn't heard from me. When I finally spoke to my mom and grandmother, it was decided that I needed to move back home and I was going to live with my grandmother for a while.

Before I moved up there, I had met this guy at the alternative high school I was sent to that although I did my dirt in Wayne County, I was madly in love with him. He and I were so bad for each other but it felt so good when we were together. During this time in my life, even when I was in Goldsboro, if you knew me you knew about him. No one on either sides of our families wanted us together, but we just didn't care. When I found out I was going to be living with my grandmother, she went to register me for school and the high school in town was full so I got transferred two towns over to go to school. Well, it just so happened that it was his hometown so this made me extra excited because I just knew for sure that we would be able to see each other more.

Also living with my grandmother, I was able to rekindle my relationship with some of my favorite cousins. We ate the roads up clubbing just about every weekend. You couldn't tell us we weren't some bad chicks. We would go out and just cut up. We fought hard and loved harder. I wasn't always the easiest to get along with because I had a smart mouth and sometimes I didn't know when to just shut up, but we had some good times together. There was this whole in the wall club we use to go to when we didn't go to the city, but the thing is, for it to be a hole in the wall, celebrities stayed coming down there. Back then is when there was a lot of territorial beefs. People did not like each other just because of the city they represented. There was always a fight going on and more times than not, my cousins and I ended up in some shape, form, or fashion. I remember this one night, there was a girl that use to hang with us running her mouth off to my boyfriend. This night one of my cousins didn't come out with us but she let me borrow her brand new white platform shoes.

So, I already mentioned we in the country and it is a hole in the wall establishment right? I got into a fight that night with the girl running her mouth. It was also the first time I had ever been maced. This girl took off all her clothes except her bra and underwear to fight me. Needless to say, she did me a favor getting undressed because it made it easier to whoop that tail, but my cousin that let me borrow the shoes was so mad at me. I still laugh about it because she did not care about nothing else. She had made me promise before we even left the house to take care of her shoes that she did not want me to wear. So I will say to my cousin, because I know one day she will read this, "Babe, I am so sorry I scuffed your shoes".

During one of the many breakups with my boyfriend, I starting seeing this guy privately that I hooked up with at the club. I don't even know why we called ourselves keeping it a secret because at the time neither one of us was dating anyone.

Eventually it all came out but again, not at first. So we had been messing around for a while when I was having a late night chat with one of my cousins and I told her about him. She verified who I was talking about and then let me know she was pimping him too. We both thought this was the funniest thing in the world. She told me to get every last dollar out of him I could. We use to call each other and let the other know we had just finished our time with him and what his location was. For the longest time he didn't know we knew but eventually he learned the joke was on him.

Chapter Nine
Christina's Pain Continues

I ended up getting pregnant with my second child when I was eighteen. I went through so many changes while pregnant with her I have no idea how to explain what all happened in the course of just nine months.

Funny story happened once while walking around the neighborhood with my sister cousin, as I called her. There was this house on corner down from my parents' house that this huge dog lived at. Well, you would think I knew about this massive sized beast and would not of been afraid to walk past the house. On our way back we passed the house and we saw the dog on the porch but paid it no mind. It was when we got near the gate that he left his spot and started charging towards us that life got real scary. Although he did not leave the gate, his loud bark and the speed at which he was running did not convince us that he was restrained. We both started running. Well she started running, mine was more of a hobble, hop, run, skip in a fast motion. I was holding my swelling belly as my life began flashing before my eyes. It was when we realized we were running from ourselves that we started laughing and could not stop. What I did not tell you was this, the reason we were on the way back to the house was because I had to pee. Well, if you have not guessed by now, I ended up peeing on myself. The more I tried to squeeze my legs together to stop it, the more that came out. She will not let me live the end of that down to this day. But I have to admit that it was pretty funny, after the fact.

I also recommitted my life to Christ at this time. I started going to church and was faithful in my walk to be the best of my ability. I asked God to forgive me and I was at peace with having yet another child out of wedlock, this time with the father denying both me and my unborn baby at the time. My relationship with my family began to heal and things were going well, until I decided that I wanted to forgive my child's father. I know that my mother just wanted the best for me and she did not want to see me hurt, but the way that she conveyed this did not help me understand it anymore. Because I chose to deal with him, I basically had to choose between him and her and that was to me, an unfair ultimatum to give me considering the circumstances.

Being connected to someone that you feel you are deeply in love with and one that you are also bringing a new life into the world with, the last thing you want to do is listen to someone telling you not to have anything to do with this person. Granted I know now if the message had been given in a way that I could of received it a lot of heartbreak could have been avoided, I once again was entering the love hate relationship she and I had for years because of her making me decide who I wanted in my child's life between her and my child's father.

I had my second child when I was nineteen years old. It was then that I think the most trifling season of my life began. I became an exotic dancer around that time and I also spent a summer in jail for probation violation after being arrested for embezzlement from the local grocery store I was working at.

During my time as a stripper once again I was faced with the power of the sexual spirit that was living inside of me. By this time I clearly had picked up a couple of more demons but this one was there during a lot of my life from childhood until I was finally delivered. While dancing, I saw that in that world it didn't matter who you were, money and nudity went a long way. I ended up telling my parents that I did it because I knew they were going to hear it anyway. Although I didn't live at home, I just wanted them to hear it from me. So, there was this one night at the club we danced at there happened to be quite a few cousins and childhood friends there. Relative or not, if they waved the money I went to the table.

Some of my most paid private dances came from people that, in actuality should have been dragging me up out of the club. The mindset that I had at the time was if they didn't care, neither did I. The hold to go and lose myself in that world was so strong, I even left my daughter home alone one night. She wasn't even a year old. Actually she was real young because she was still in a crib and she wasn't at the pull up on the bar age yet now that I think about it. I gave her some Tylenol to put her to sleep and locked up my house and left. One of my cousins asked me where she was and I lied and told her she was at her father's house with her grandmother. During that time, her grandmother was known to keep her a lot so I wasn't questioned when I said it. When I got home late that night, I ran in the house and checked on her to make sure she was okay and that she was still breathing. The very next month, an apartment out there in the building next to mine burned down. It was the same apartment as mine just a different building. My apartment number was 310 and it was apartment 410. So many people came to my house looking for me and my daughter that night. I remember the concern from people that I didn't even realize that I had impacted. The news wasn't clear on what apartment it was and from looking at the media coverage you would of thought it was mine. Even now I look like wow God, I so didn't deserve that but yet again, even in my mess, I recognize that He was covering me.

I was so consumed with guilt for leaving my daughter the month before and I never did it again, I always felt bad about it and kept that shame to myself for years.

There was another incident during my exotic dancing phase that as sinful as I was living, I know that there is a God and He was watching over me. This incident is what made me start taking someone with me when I went places. I never really had an issue of going out by myself to do my dirt until the night I realized just how close to death I was placing myself in these situations. For some people, it only takes them one time and they learn their lessons, but for me, not so much. Again I had placed my drink down in a bar full of people. I did not think of it as being dangerous because everyone loved me, at least they smiled at me like they did. The next morning when I woke up with a stranger beside me in a bed I had never seen and another man naked on the floor, this did not even scare me. It was when I walked past the other bedroom and saw the girl in there with the guys shaking her and smacking her and the blood on the sheets before the door slammed in my face that I got worried. Luckily for me, who am I kidding, it was not luck, but one of the guys threw what I called the young one some keys and told him to drop me off.,

    Her father and I also entered into what I later learned was an abusive relationship. Although I always threw the first punch, we began to fight a lot and it was very unhealthy for the both of us. I would call the police and no sooner than his parents would get him out of jail he would be right back at my apartment and we would be right back at it. We had a hold on each other that just can not be explained and it took almost sixteen years before I was finally delivered of it.

    During this time, I was still stripping but only because the bills needed to be paid. He use to beg me to quit and I use to tell him if he could put the money in the house that I was making that I would.

My family took bus trips to New York every July 4th weekend. It was tradition, we would go up there and for Labor Day they would come down here. Remember the year the rapper ODB from Wu Tang Clan ran away from the hospital? Well he ran straight to the hotel we were staying at in Staten Island. So many things happened that weekend but that was one of the funniest. We had celebrity encounters all that weekend. When we first got there while we were checking into our rooms I went to use the bathroom.

While I was in there one of my cousins and another cousin's boyfriend came in there while I was in there. They walked in begging me to be quiet and whispering trying to convince me to come to their room to give them a private strip show. The level of respect was clearly gone because of the profession that I was in and I didn't have any for them since they didn't have any for me. I cursed them so far out I am still surprised that no one realized what was going on. I was just angry about it. They backed out the bathroom and it wasn't mentioned anymore. Truth be told, it just wasn't mentioned anymore that weekend. It wasn't the last time relatives came on to me under the blanket of can you just do a show for us. And after a while, I stopped saying no.

*****

When my daughter was six months old I moved into my first apartment. I was so excited to finally be on my own and have a place that I could set my own rules. Because I had been staying with my boyfriend's family when I moved, he moved in with us because he had gotten use to having us around everyday. For a while it was a good fit. I was working at a well known grocery store in town and he had a job at the factory up the street.

One day while at work, I decided there was some stuff that I just had to have for my apartment and for my kids. I could of easily asked for the necessities like milk and diapers, but it was the coloring books and candles and other items that I wanted to get on my own. Needless to say I got caught smuggling groceries and was arrested. I went to jail for embezzlement charges which were later lessoned to misdemeanor larceny and I was placed on probation. The beginning of a downward spiral began after my boyfriend and I started fighting and for a while I couldn't find another job.

One night while in the bathroom the spirit of suicide came over me very strong. I looked in the mirror and I did not see myself. I can not describe what I saw but I will try my best to do so now. Looking back at me I could see myself behind my own eyes. The face in the mirror resembled mine but it was much more menacing than the cute face I was accustomed to. On the inside I was being tormented and I know I felt miserable but the face was smiling, sneering even. I was not talking but the face was talking to me. It was telling me to end it all. The face, my face told me that I should kill myself. I then saw two dark shadowy figures standing over my left and my right shoulders and they both were telling me different methods to use. The light was on in the bathroom, but it was so dark. I could see myself but I was surrounded by a dim red light. The time was around midnight, I remember because a television show called The Wire had just started and there was a repeat on. I picked up the phone and I called the Bishop of the church I was a member of at the time. I cried and told him that I was being tormented and that I really needed him to pray for me.

The response that I got was not the one I expected. He told me that I needed to call my biological father and ask him to pray for me. I was in total shock. First of all, demons were literally chasing me and I was in dire need of spiritual guidance and he put me off because of what I felt like it was a late hour that I called. Later in my life I would learn difference between hirelings and called shepherds of a flock and at that moment although I did not know it, he was showing his true colors as a hireling.

I ended up singing songs of praise and just asking God to come see me and help me. I told him that although I was a sinner, I knew who He was and I believed if He said the word, those demons would have to leave me alone. I fell asleep that night in perfect peace, and never thought any more about it. I did stop going to that church. I visited from time to time but I lost my respect for the leadership and the church itself after that. About a year later, the Bishop saw me at my sister's then boyfriend's mother house and asked me why I had left the church. I reminded him of that night and in a voice mocking his own, I told him the response he gave me when I called for help. He never asked me anything again.

The morning of June 26, 1999 I was laying in bed with my daughter's father when there was a knock at the door. No one knew he was there because it was after one of the many times that I had had him arrested for one of our domestic disputes so we were pretending for the sake of the courts that we didn't have any communication with each other. I opened the door and a Sheriff's Deputy that I knew very well was standing on the other side. "Peanut, I am here to take you in". The words didn't really register when he said them. I asked him if he would give me a second to go put some clothes on and throw my ponytail on my head, in which he did. I really thought I was just going downtown and that I would be back. I did come back, but not until forty five days later.

While I was in jail, just like when I was in the mental hospital I met some interesting people. I learned that women are really nasty while I was locked up as well. The hardest part about being incarcerated though was the deaths that happened to people I was extremely close with and I was not in a position to even attend their funerals. The father of my childhood best friend lost his life and then there was my little boyfriend as I called him, one of the babies that went to preschool with my daughter, he died as well. I found out about his death in the most unorthodox way. We were watching television in the common area and the breaking news flash interrupted the show we were watching. The news announced the story of a house fire on the street near my apartment that some of my closest friends lived on. They showed a picture of the house that instantly sprung to my mind when I heard the name of the area. I was in denial even as I went to the phone that it was where I thought it was. I called my daughter's grandmother and asked her if it was true. I know her response was yes because the next thing I remember was letting out this piercing scream that I didn't even realize was coming from my mouth and several of the inmates that I had befriended were picking me up off the floor. I cried and I cried. They ended up taking me out of the pod and putting me in the gymnasium by myself. Someone gave me a pack of cigarettes, which I wasn't even smoking at the time, and a lighter and left me alone with my grief. I lit the cigarette and took a pull while thinking of the thick blunts I used to smoke before I came in here. Either my mind was that gone or the smoke really was that strong because it calmed me and I felt like I was floating enough that the tears sustained and I was able to just pray that everyone else was okay despite the death of my five year old little friend. Just days after his death, I learned that my childhood friend had lost his life in an automobile accident.

By His Stripes

By this time I was just numb with grief and instead of tears memories flooded my mind of the last time I was with them. We were preparing to watch our favorite show Beverly Hills 90210 and we were getting ready also to have dinner prepared by the mother of his child. He did not want eggs in his salad so that was a funny argument and also I was trying my best to convince him that my middle name would be the perfect for his unborn daughter. Funny how you remember details of the most tragic moments in your life no matter how long ago that they occur. Then later that week, yet another friend died. This guy was really like my little brother for real. Whenever he came into town although he would stay at my apartment, I later figured out just his clothes stayed there because he was always on the go. The weekend that he was shot, he was supposed to be staying at my house, but because I was in jail he couldn't come. He lost his life in the most senseless way. The story goes that he lost it on the basketball court over an argument that was petty. Isn't that how it usually goes though? A gun is brought to a verbal fight that is just not that serious? That was three funerals I had to miss because of my decisions that landed me where I was. The obituaries ended up getting mailed to me, but that did not help my pain of not being able to bid my farewells to my friends.

Chapter Ten
Christina's Rejection

While I was in jail, much to my and his families objection, my daughter's father and I had started yet once again rekindling our relationship. It was planned that when I got out, I would be coming to their house and there would be this big cookout for me and a celebration. Somewhere between that plan and my release date those plans changed. This girl came in from the area we lived and she was bragging about her sexual exploits with him and telling me of other women that was getting in on the action. Honestly that was not even the part that got to me. What got me was the fact that this girl was just disgusting. I can not say much more about her nice so I will leave it at that. I know you may be thinking that she could have been lying right? Well, she not only proved her case but when I spoke to him he could not even deny it because of the details that she had revealed. This man sat on the phone and tried to play me for stupid with the "it just happened excuses". That was the end of that rekindled flame, at least for that time.

Not too long after my release, I still had my apartment, but I just did not want to stay in it. I would go home and get clothes and leave again for days at a time. During this time, I would go stay at one of my cousin's houses because the neighborhood that they lived in was the center of everything.

One day, I was driving back to the house when I drove past a funeral home that was packed beyond capacity with people. All I saw was the men. There were light ones, dark ones, brown ones, and tan ones. My mouth began to water with excitement at the pleather of men I could have my pick from. Never mind the fact that they were at a funeral home, that did not matter to me. It also did not matter to me that I did not know these people and that they were grieving. I just saw an open buffet for me to go and feed the monster that was still living inside of me. I went to my cousin house and changed my clothes.

While I was getting dressed, one of my cousins came and asked me where I was going. I told them and they could not do anything but laugh because they knew I was so serious. When I got back to the funeral home, my first stop was to view the body and sign the guest book. I needed a name to go with the deceased and even more so, I was going to need to see who were most of the guests there so I could come up with my story of how we knew each other and justify my being there. It did not take long to discover that there were a lot of well known drug dealers and pimps there and seeing as how this was a world I knew very well, I was able to jump right in. I ended up with one of the deceases brothers. I was so good, or should I say that seducing spirit was so good, I ended up leaving my car for someone else to drive from the funeral home and I rode with him back to the family house for the recessional. We had an awesome two week affair before we got bored with each other and he realized that I did not listen very well and he did not want to deal with me anymore. They were used to telling girls what to do and who to do it to and I was just not one that could follow directions. Crazy as that time was and truth be told as dangerous as it was, during that moment, I just thought it was something to do.

One day while sitting on my cousin's front steps a blue Cadillac pulled up and one of the guys at the house went out and was talking to the occupants. I heard the driver call my name and I went to see who it was just to learn it was a former classmate of mine. So after we exchanged hellos and hugs he told me that the passenger wanted to holler at me. I knew that the driver was a local dope boy and he only hung out with get money guys so both my greed and my sexual appetite obliged to his request. We exchanged numbers and he promised to call me later and I did not think anything else about it. I went up the street to another guy house that I had met at a club a couple of years earlier. He was one of the neighborhood weed suppliers and I knew that he was crushing on me hard. The only thing that stopped us from hooking up was the fact that he was in a wheelchair. He had been shot and was paralyzed from the waste down so although he had money, he was not my type because he could not supply my real need.

By His Stripes

The story behind how we met though was too funny. My family and I were out at a club downtown one night and I was on the dance floor feeling all eyes on me when I turned and saw him and his chair posted up on the side of the floor. His boys had since left him and were around the club getting there on *macks* on and I guess he was hindering their floor. Well me being me, I decided to go over and give him a lap dance. I was just grinding on him and smiling and making him feel real good. So we became friends after that. So back to the story, I was at his house dipping in supply when my beeper went off. I did not recognize the number so I called back. It was the passenger of the Cadillac! I told him I would meet up with him later and he said he would come get me just let him know when I was ready.

The first couple of days we were together I thought were great. Although it was weird that he really did not like to leave the house and I later learned he hardly ever went out during the day, I felt I could deal with it. He also introduced me to the white powdery substance known as cocaine. He and I would get high together and then we would feed our bodies with each other. This went on for weeks before it hit me who he was. Although I heard his name a couple of times and I knew the guy he was hanging with when we met was a former classmate, it did not hit me until I saw a picture of him with his ex and their kids that I realized that not only was she a former classmate, but I considered her a friend at the time.

By now, we were already well into a relationship, as unhealthy as it was and I did not see the point in leaving. It was not going to change the fact that I was with him. When she found out it was me she was so angry. I know she hated me and the things she wanted to do to me out of the hurt and betrayal she felt were easily understood considering the circumstance. But what could I do about it? Also at the time, he hated her and loved me, so he would threaten her with each threat that she sent to me. Things got really out of hand with that and to this day I haven't seen her but I was really sorry that it happened like that.

The longer I was with him, the more possessive he became. I ended up giving up my apartment to live with him full time and he moved me into what I now call the house of horrors. Every night we got high and every night we ended up fighting. The fact that I fought back turned him on and made him love me even more according what he said, but I know now that was not love. He would talk about the women before me and how they use to treat him in the bedroom and remind me of how I would never meet their standards. He talked about this one particular girl all the time and how all his friends had her. They would just send her from room to room to satisfy their every need. The way he talked about her I thought surely she would never be a threat to me if she was to come around, but I was so wrong.

I had a job at the local movie rental place during the day when he should have been sleeping considering our episodes that we had at night, but because I wasn't in the house, he could not sleep. He would come and sit in the parking lot and call inside the store and ask me who was the man I was talking to when in actuality I was just ringing up a customer. He would get mad if he couldn't see me from the window when I walked to go check the shelves or went to the back of the store to do something and he would call in yelling at whoever answered the phone out of anger for covering for me. Eventually my boss told me it was not going to work out and that he would have to let me go. He was so happy.

 The day I was fired we rode around looking for the girl that he and his friends liked to share. He wanted her to come to the house that night, supposedly just to party and chill with the guy that was staying with us. We actually found her and she came over. I instantly did not like her. When we got back to the house, I went into the master bedroom to sulk and wait for him to come in so that we could argue. After a few minutes when he didn't come in behind me, I went to see what was taking so long. He was upstairs in one of the bedrooms having sex with her. I could not believe that he would disrespect me like that. Yes, I thought that was disrespectful and not the fact that he had just got me fired from my job. See, him getting me fired from my job made me feel like he really loved me and he just couldn't be without me. I stomped back into the bedroom with my tears and heartache to wait for him to come back down. When he walked in the room he thought it was the funniest thing ever that I felt the way I did. He told me that she was just a pass around and that I was the one he was with so it should not have mattered. He apologized and gave me a bag of cocaine and walked out. While I was sitting there she came in.

At this point, I had already believed that my status was better than hers so I was not even mad anymore. She sat on the bed with me and asked if I would share my treats with her. I gave her some and she asked me had I ever smoked a cigarette with cocaine in it before. I told her no and watched her in amazement as she mixed the tobacco and the white powder together and in no time flat had the cigarette lit. I was a little apprehensive about smoking it. Something about smoking it made me feel like it was worse than sniffing it so I passed. He walked in and immediately was angered at the smell. I guess he knew it all too well and he *spazed* out on her and threw her out and told one of our houseguests to take her back where they had got her from. Then his anger turned on me. He called me all sorts of names. I tried to tell him that I did not smoke any but he did not believe me. He drug me out the bed and tossed me on the floor. Instantly I sprung back up and charged him with all my might. This only angered him more and he began to land punches that should of knocked me out but I kept fighting. At some point I fell and he pulled me into the closet. It was then that I got scared. The closet was were he kept all his guns and they were never on safety. I knew he was just going to try to beat me with it, but I was terrified as to what could of happen if he had. I started screaming for my life and I guess the person in the living room couldn't take it anymore because he came and intervened. He was laughing as he grabbed his boy off me and reminding us that we loved each other and we should not of been acting like that. They left me in the closet and I sat there for hours before my lover returned with tears in his eyes to beg me not to leave him. He apologized for what had happened and promised that it would not happen again. He told me that it angered him to see me with a laced cigarette and that he did not want me to end up like that girl. How ironic, huh?

I had already moved in and all my stuff from my apartment was there, so moving out would not have been as easily said as done. So I stayed. It was during this time that my son was with his father and my daughter was with me there for a little while, but eventually I abandoned her somewhere safer than the environment I was living in. One day, after one of our many arguments, his mother got mad at me about something and she decided since her name was on the house, she wanted me out. While I was gone, she had his friends put all my stuff on the back deck. All my furniture and photos and irreplaceable memories were thrown out like trash. When I went back and saw it outside I didn't even try to go into the house.

While I was staring at disbelief and digging in my rubble of mess trying to get stuff out the rain began to fall. It wasn't just a light rain either. The rain drops were big as gallon buckets being poured out and they all fell on my stuff. My daughter's baby book was out there and I remember that being the thing that I really wanted to find before it was destroyed. I couldn't find it and I had become hysterical while searching so I had to stop seeing as how my vision was blurry from tears and the rain.

My parents lived about ten minutes from the house of horrors and I went there out of just needing to feel some sense of comfort. At first no one came to the door, but one of my sisters came and I just cried and cried and cried. I grieved for the stuff that I lost and not the mess I had become. Even after all of that, I still went back to him.

We ended up moving in with his grandfather and picked up right where we left off. His mother still hated me and she was even more mad at the fact that I was still in the picture. I did not care. During this time there were people that owed him money and I was starting to see what happened to people that he did not care about it. It was nothing compared to the abuse I suffered. In my mind it made sense that he did not do me like that so he must care for me. One night we went out and loaded half the guns in the house in the car. Fortunately we did not find who he was looking for, but he was not going to come home with spending bullets. The first stop we made was in an area where there were a lot of green utility boxes and power sources for the city. They shot them out with the machine guns and uzis until all the magazines were spent. In the midst of the sparks flying and the bullets ringing out I just prayed one did not ricochet and hit me. I will never forget a gun was placed in my hand. My target was in toward some houses where an enemy was known to rest his head. Never mind the fact that there could have been children in the house or even the houses around it, I had to prove my loyalty by shooting. I remember praying for the best and pointing the gun slightly towards the sky hoping the bullet did not reach one soul, but at least my life was safe and I proved I was down for the cause.

The more I was there the jealous spirit and insecure spirit that he had did not want me to leave his sight even to go to the bathroom. I recall laying beside him and moving to go to the bathroom and the click of the gun under his pillow followed by him asking where I was going would stop me in my tracks. I could only take a shower when he took one and he could go a couple of days without. My life had become such a mess. When I finally glanced in the mirror I saw a shell of who I use to be. I literally was the walking dead.

I decided that I did not want this anymore. He had already told me that if I ever left him he would kill my family and then me. He told me he would make me watch him do it. He reminded me that my kids hardly saw me and since they were happy where they were, they would not miss me. He told me I was his and that

I could not leave him. "You know how you feel about your sisters" he would say. Each time I looked like I was plotting to leave he would bring up that he had nothing to lose and if he could not have me no one could have me. He told me the police would not take him without a fight and the look in his eyes when he spoke those words convinced me he was not lying. I believed him because based on everything I had already seen and experienced with him, I knew he meant every word he spoke.

The day I decided to leave I just did not care about the threats. I did not want anything to happen to my family but the promises of killing them and then killing me sounded better than the situation I was in. In my mind, I thought that it wouldn't be so bad because at least I would be here on earth without them. As I told him goodbye and turned to walk out the house I did not even hear him come up behind me. I did not see his fist coming towards my face as I reached for the doorknob. I did hear the crack of the bone in my jaw at the impact of his hand. Usually, I would of fought back, but this time I decided to run. I got the door open and I ran. I ran as hard and as fast as I could to the house up the road that was home to the most unlikeliest source of help. I ran to his mother. She opened the door and instantly looked at my frame and my face and told me I needed to go home. She told me she loved her son and my life depended on what I decided at that moment. I went to my parents house and told them if they did not let me come back I would die. I told them I was tired of the drugs and I was tired of the abuse. I begged them to let me come get myself together and they felt and saw I truly meant it. For a while, I actually did.

While my fractured jaw healed during one of my most favorite times of the year, I could not eat seeing as how I couldn't chew. It was painful to be around so much food and not be able to enjoy any of it. It was even harder to see the look in my family members eyes as they had to look at the living carcass I had become during my run with the man I had just left.

Chapter Eleven
Christina's Whirlwind

A few months after that I got a job at the gas station around the corner from my mother and father's house. I also started dating again but not as focused on it as I was before. While working at the gas station I got another job right next door at a food fast restaurant but that did not last long once I saw how nasty they were and I started telling customers to go somewhere else to eat. So I stayed at the gas station and got in good with management. Although the hours were horrible and I sometimes walked home late at night by myself while closing up the store, it was a price I was willing to pay to get back on my feet and prove that I really wanted to do right this time. I ended up going to the local community college to get my GED while working there. What I failed to mention earlier in my story is how I dropped out of high school two months before graduation. I have my cap and gown pictures and everything, but I did not walk across the stage. That June, I signed up for classes and began studying for the exam while I was at work. I ended up not taking classes at all once I learned I could just test and as long as I scored a certain number, I could move on to the next test. I opted for that choice. I ended up passing the GED exam number thirty seven out of the five hundred and forty three people that took it that year. When I got my credentials in the mail my sisters and I jumped up and down and anxiously awaited that November for the graduation ceremony. I ended up not going. Other than my sisters, no one remembered my accomplishment. They begged me to go but I did not see the point seeing as how no one would be there. They forgot they would have needed a ride themselves and since my parents weren't going it was pointless to me. It would be over a decade later that my dad would tell me he did not even know I had my GED, he thought for years that I was just a high school drop out.

Once again it was time for me to run away from my problems. This time I ran to the arms of a *R&B* singer look alike who was just as in love with me as I with him. Remember the crooner Jon B? Yea, he looked just like him. He got me a job waitressing at the diner he was the chef at and we made that work until I grew tired of him.

I started back dating a guy who started off as a nickel and dime drug dealer but had since grown to be a local area supplier. Our relationship had always been based on friendship so I thought so it was nothing to pick up where we left off with each other. The thing that sucked with our encounter though was he constantly had people in his ear. Where as I was really looking out for his best interest, he thought I only wanted him for the money so we had a lot of disagreements. While we rekindled our flame, the annual trip to New York came back around and I decided to go. I had an awesome time as usual and there was this guy that I had hooked up with years before that took care of me while I was up there. He was a relative of a relative so I hid under the cover of we cousins to excuse our time together. He truly knew me as no one else did and he always told me what I needed to hear and not just what I wanted to hear. It was when he stopped feeding my inner appetite that I lost interest in him. I mean don't get me wrong the friendship was awesome, but there was still that underlining issue of my sexual addiction and he was no longer fulfilling it.

My cousin was dating this girl that I at first thought was his main girl but later learned she was the side chick. But I grew extremely close to her and her family. Actually, now that I think about it, they weren't her family, they were her children's family, but they embraced her all the same and when they met me they embraced me and my daughter as well.

We had some fun. Once you get in the church, you are told that you were delivered from a miserable life of sin, but truth be told I was not miserable at this point in my life. I was a Criminal Justice major, I had a job, I had a car, and I had my place. I felt like I was on top of my game again. My sister Tiffany had just started going to the University of North Carolina in Greensboro and I was able to help her out, so I thought life was good.

I was newly single again so I really thought I was hot stuff. My boyfriend had moved out, he could not handle the independence that I had developed. He was not even man enough to break up with me though. He waited until I left to go to school one morning to put his plan into action. I left school and went to my Godmother's house to get my hair done before going home. Mind you when I left the house that morning, he was in the bed, and he mentioned nothing of the sort to give me a clue he was leaving. I thought it was just a normal day.

When I got home that afternoon, the first thing I noticed was tire marks in the grass in my front yard. This had me cussing in itself because my landlord was really particular about this house, and my boyfriend knew that. I couldn't figure out which of his friends he had let come and do that. I went in the house read to flip out and what I found when I opened the door will always be etched in my brain. My house that was once completely furnished was now empty. My daughter's room was the only room that had anything in it. The couches, televisions, bed, even the pillows was gone. He had taken everything his drug selling dollar had purchased. I really do not remember how long I stood there. It felt like hours but it was probably just seconds. At the time I was driving what was called a "head truck".

You know when crack heads lend out there vehicles for weeks at a time for drugs? Yea, I had one of those. I know I got back in the truck and I was crying. I could not believe he did that. I was playing our last conversation over in my head and I remembered I had been doing homework and he kept taunting me calling me "college girl". He kept telling me how special I thought I was. As I started driving, I was not sure where I was going, but as it turned out, I was headed straight for his grandmother's house. I knew that was the only place he would go when he called himself leaving.

While on the road, I still do not understand how I did not get pulled over. I know I had to be going at least ninety five miles per hour which was well over the speeding limit. It had started drizzling with rain on my way there. When I pulled up on the country dirt road that his family lived on the first thing I saw was a U-Haul truck. It was not even the truck itself that sent me further over the edge. That I do know. It was when I saw all his friends sitting and standing around it smoking, drinking, and laughing. It was also when I saw his supposed to have been ex girlfriend standing there with them that I lost it. According to eye witnesses, I accelerated and came into the yard and ran into his Jeep Cherokee. BOOM! They said that I backed up and ran into it again. BOOM! The story goes that I kept doing this until he came running outside and when he did I turned the truck I was driving on him. One of his cousins grabbed him and they both jumped behind a tree just in the nick of time. And at this point, the poor truck I was driving could not take anymore. It idled out and died. It is so funny how they say I jumped out of the truck and ran towards him ready for war. I am just three quarters of an inch shy of being five feet five inches tall. My ex stood at six feet I think six inches and was not a small framed man. His ex was a giant of a woman as well and I did not see her coming but one of our mutual friends tells me that when I slowly turned around and looked up at her standing over me I politely let her know she was in danger and she might want to move. They say she did, I did not give her time to answer because I had turned my attention back to him.

I guess somewhere in the midst of all this the police was called. When they pulled up, my ex was screaming how he wanted them to take me to jail. The officer took his statement and placed me in the front seat of the squad car. I kind of remember him talking to me for the ride but not really. I do know he did not take me to jail. I know he took me home first and when he saw it, he asked if there was someone else that could be with me. I had him take me around the corner to one of my cousins' house. When we pulled up, I got out and walked in while she was walking out to find out what was going on. She had seen us come through her window. The officer explained to her, as she later told me that my mindset did not belong in jail, but I would have to go to court.

Can you believe the case was thrown out? I think it helped my case that he and I had already reconnected by my court date. I was actually driving the rental car he had while he was waiting on repairs of his truck that I had wrecked. The judge had me stand before him and I asked if I could speak on my behalf before sentencing. I let him know that my ex and I were no longer exes and that we had gotten back together. The judge's response was the fact that he did not know whether to say congratulations or that the guy was a fool, but he threw it out. Still can't believe to this day he dismissed the charges, although the charge of Injury to Personal Property went on my record, he still dismissed it.

Hanging with my cousin's non-girlfriend once again, I met some interesting people. I know you reading this and may say why does she always say that, but that is the only word I know to describe the people I came in contact with. By now, I had picked my cocaine habit back up be it as discreet as I thought it was. I would only share this part of my life with certain people and my new family were the ones I shared it with. It wasn't as bad as it was before, I only did it every now and then, but doing it is doing it all the same.

I think I fit in with them so well because I was loud and opinionated just like them, and so was my daughter who was like three going on four at the time. I was not afraid to stand on what I believed even if I was the only one standing, and I did not take any mess from anybody. Plus again, there is just that lovable factor I mentioned before, you either going to love me or hate me. There wasn't anyone that they introduced me to that did not connect with me. My boldness to say that I was who I was and still be taking care of my business also was a plus on my side.

I had started doing a little bit of stripping on the side again. Just for the extra money and just because truth be told, at that time, I still had it. I would get set up with shows where there were NBA players, lawyers, doctors, and just prominent men in the community. I would go to my parents house and give my sisters one to two hundred dollars a piece just because every week. I would tell them not to tell where they got it from and to this day we laugh at how they had all this money but no way to go spend it. I was not living smart with the money I was making. Just as soon as I made it, I blew it or gave it away. I wanted everyone around me to be happy and have something.

One night, I was out with my cousin's girl and we were getting high all night long plotting our next move. We smoked blunt after blunt and did some lines as well. When the drugs ran out, I prepared to make the twenty minute drive home. There was no need for me to stay any longer, there was nothing else to do. While I was walking out she had disappeared into one of the many rooms in the apartment and right before I reached the kitchen to head out the door she called me back and asked if I wanted to hit the blunt before I left. Seeing as how we had been smoking marijuana all night, I naturally assumed that this is what it was. I said yea, sure, and grabbed the blunt from her hand and deeply inhaled while walking into the room she was in. When I blew the smoke out I realized my tongue and my lips had gone numb and all at the same time she was being told to hurry up and close the door to keep the smell in. These things happened in a matter of seconds and in those seconds I also realized my friend had just introduced me to crack cocaine.

My heart broke into a million pieces. I did not know she smoked the real stuff as we called it. She did not even give me the option of choosing if I wanted to or not. I was so angry. I said a few choice words and I left. Our friendship was never the same again after that. I still spoke but the trust was gone. I thank God to this day that I did not become addicted. I thank Him that was the first and the last time that happened to me. I also thank Him that that was the only thing that the blunt was laced with that night.

Another trip to New York sent me on a shopping spree in Manhattan. There was this boutique there with prices just unbelievable so I naturally came home with three times as much stuff as I went up there with. My first weekend home my best friend and I decided to hook up with our girl and her boyfriend and head out to the club. We were they type of chicks that looked like we would be stuck up when we walked in, but once we hit the dance floor all standards that had been preset over us were thrown out. While out we started planning our trip to that year's Black Bike Week at Myrtle Beach, South Carolina. It was decided that two of us would drive down later in the week and meet our friend down who would go before us to meet her boyfriend and spend some time with him first.

I was taking Neurontin pills from a diagnosis of Bipolar Disorder and taking them with a Corona beer made me feel extra good. We took my car down there and since I didn't have to drive I popped a happy pill as I called them opened a beer and prepared for the ride. When we arrived it was late and we parked in the parking lot and went into the hotel to go to bed, intending on getting up early in the morning to go to the office to check in. When we awoke the next day, we could here a commotion outside and after a brief investigation by my friend, she came running back in to get my car keys because they were towing cars without stickers. I tossed her my keys and then proceeded to look for something to put on so I could go outside. While she was cranking my car up, a tow truck pulled behind my car and would not move. He was trying to block her in so they could tow my car. At that moment I could only think of the fact that I was in South Carolina and there was no way I was going to be trapped down here. I ran out the door and down the stairs and jumped on the hood of my car. I started chanting about how I was not going to come down or something to that sort. The police ended up getting called and I still refused to come down. There were people call over coming out their rooms and watching as every available cop on the strip came to see about this girl on top of a car that would not come down.

My friend's boyfriend ended up paying the tow company not to tow my car to just end the spectacle and I became an instant celebrity for about four hours and was known around the beach as the girl on top of the car.

Not too long after we came back from the beach, two other friends joined our circle and out of nowhere we started clubbing hard. What I mean by hard is Thursday thru Sunday we were out at the club. We called ourselves Fab Five and we were *badder* than bad. We each had a different personality but we all complimented each other. In a year's time we hit every bar there was to hit, so much so that at one point I even had a drink named after me at one of the clubs we frequented. Yes, you could go to the bartender and ask him to make you a "Christina" and he would. It was so funny to see the faces of my haters when they would hear the drink being ordered and no explanation needed for the ingredients.

For a while we went hard and broke hearts even harder. We were just busy being cute and we loved it. The following year when Memorial Day came back around again, we decided that Black Bike Week was overrated and we decided to just go to Atlanta for the weekend instead. At the time every last one of us was connected to a dope boy and we all made our own money working so money was not an option. We left to enjoy ourselves and treated Atlanta like our own little Vegas. We know what happens in Vegas stays in Vegas, so I will apply the same rules to our Atlanta trip. I will say this, I do not know what the food is like now, but we went to eat at Justin's Restaurant and we all ordered something different and I still have temptations to call and see if they will overnight me a plate via FedEx. It was so good.

I was the driver on the way back in town and I was getting it. We almost made it back in like three maybe three and half hours, but we ran into traffic. Come to find out an eighteen wheeler had caught on fire on the highway. We all took a moment to pray and reflect on life. One of my friend's step dad was a truck driver at the time so it was especially sobering for her. When we got back home it calmed us down a whole lot. As a matter of fact the we really did not club together as hard as we did. My girls and I may have slowed down, but I still was on a fast track to destruction.

I had been carrying the secret of using cocaine with me and finally shared with the man that I was dating. Considering he was one of the main suppliers for the drug in our area, I had my fair share to access the drug whenever I wanted to. Although he and I had a love and hate relationship and there was never a guarantee that the love side would last past a week, we had that in common and it was the dysfunctional glue that kept us together.

I still had VIP access to some of the major mostly Caucasian crowd clubs in the area, so I would still go out and get my party just as hard as I did when Fab Five rolled out together. Every now and then the girls and I would hook up and paint the town, but mostly for events and concerts so it was far and few in between. I started rekindling my close relationship with one of my cousins and she and I started running just as hard as we could if for no other reason other than to make our boyfriends mad at the time.

I shared my secret with her one night while we were out and she let me know she had never tried it, but had thought about it. I did not want to be the one to give her first experience, but I would of rather it be with me than with someone who did not care about her. So we went into a stall in the bathroom and we both decided to go into the bag together. Although I was using, I was not a heavy user. I could ration the gram or two gram bag that my boyfriend gave me and make it last until the next week. I used only what was needed to help me switch to whatever character I wanted to be for the night. After a couple of weekends, we brought another friend out to the club with us one weekend.

During one of our sneaky trips to the bathroom to get our toot on, our friend came and knocked on the door wanting to come in with us. We looked at each other trying to figure out if we wanted to let her in or not, and finally my cousin was like, let her in, she going to have to join the club though. We figured if she participated, our secret was safe. This turned out to be true, but unfortunately she was not as strong minded as we were and the drug had more control over her than she over it.

After a month or so, we noticed that every time we went out, our friend either wanted it or she already had it. Well, seeing as how I was drinking and I was smoking marijuana, I did not have to have it to party every weekend. Watching her self destruct reminded me of how I was years earlier and it also sobered not only me, but my cousin up as well. We no longer wanted to do it and we felt so bad for introducing her to the drug. Her family life started spiraling out of control. She was no longer able to feed her family. She and her husband would come to my house and I would take them grocery shopping. I even ended up giving her a car because he eventually left her and she had all those kids to get around. Our friendship slowly deteriorated and I have no idea where she is now, but I pray that she is doing okay.

When I slowed down, I slowed all the way down, I just stopped doing everything. I decided that I wanted to get married. I was twenty five years old and I wanted to be a wife. I proposed to my own again and off again lover at the time, and after some convincing he said yes. Saturday September 13, 2003 on the beaches of Charleston, South Carolina I married a man that argued with me all the way up until we said "I Do". I knew deep down in my heart we should not of married. I actually knew when a couple of nights before he told someone on the phone that since I wanted to do it and I asked he was going to do it. Even before the ceremony when I started getting cold feet, he told me seeing as how we had driven all the way down there, we were going to get married and I was to shut up talking. Looking back, even then I did not realize that my choice of relationships was so unhealthy for me. I just wanted a man to tell me he loved me and be with me for the rest of my life.

Well, the rest of my life ended about two weeks later. At the time I had this little Carolina Blue four door Honda and he went out to warm the car for me to go to work one morning. This should have been a bell of alarm ringing in my ear in itself because this was something that he never had done before. The night before I had taken my son and daughter with me to go visit friends and get my hair done. That was all we did that night and we came home and went to bed since it was fairly late when we got there. He came back in the house breathing fire out of his nostrils he was so mad. I couldn't figure out what was wrong with him and sent the kids upstairs so I could find out. He told me how he found used condoms all over my backseat and someone had told him I had sex in the car the night before. I was livid. For one, because he was out there playing eye spy and did not know me better than that than to have my children ride home sitting on what he said was sperm filled condoms. He showed me his findings, just the wrappers, but how convenient that it provided him a way out two weeks after we got married. It was years later that I learned that the condoms really were in my car. My daughter had found them and was playing with them on the way home and my son had told her to get rid of it or she would get in trouble. The only way she could do that was to stuff them in the seat. When she told me this I was so shocked. I really thought he was just doing what he usually did and looked for the door to get him out of the commitment he had made. Although this incident was not totally one that was his fault, it did not mean that once we reconciled he would not again, look for a way to close the door on our relationship.

The next weekend we drove back to Charleston, South Carolina to find out about having our vows annulled. The attorney explained that if we had gotten married under false pretenses, then we could be granted the annulment. I told the attorney he falsely pretending he wanted to be with me and that should have been good enough, but he said it was not. We would have to file for divorce like normal people.

Not even a month went by after that and he decided we would try it again. He moved back home and we set out to work on our relationship. We started clubbing together again and I even picked the bag back up. Before we went out, I would do lines of cocaine to prepare me for the world that I really wanted to leave, but to keep my marriage I was willing to go back in. I started picking up girls to bring home with us as gifts to him. I would pass it off as having a threesome, but I would always end up watching or I would get out of the bed.

Truthfully, I brought them home to do what I did not want to do. I know longer wanted to sleep with him and the girls were really a gift to me. Yes, there were times I participated, but only long enough to get my fix and then I would grab the "softball and bat" as the cocaine and straw was called and I would end my night with my drug. Sometimes the girls would get upset with me because seeing as how I was the one that lured her there, they would think they were going to be with me, but being the sweet talker that I was, I convinced them that being with my husband was being with me.

One night not long after we moved one of my cousins and her kids in for a while, he made me extremely mad. I told him I wasn't going out with him anymore and he and I needed to talk about what the problem was between us. He acted like he could not hear me. He just laid in bed as if I was not speaking and pretending to be sleep.

This caused me to see red. I stormed out the room, not sure of what I was going to do and I went down the stairs and stomped to my laundry room for the brand new bottle of Clorox that my sister and my cousin had just purchased. At the time, I did not know that it was not flammable and I also did not think about the fact that other people were in the house. I went back into my bedroom and I started pouring the Clorox all over him, all over the bed, and all over the floor. I grabbed the matches off the dresser and I started striking. I struck match after match and nothing happened. He jumped up and slid against the wall screaming at me how crazy I was and I screamed back at him how it was too late to try to talk to me now. My sister Tiffany ran in the room and she pulled me out so he could get dressed and leave. She took me downstairs where her and my cousin gave me a serious lesson on how Clorox is not flammable. He moved out that night.

Usually I would of fought to keep him there, but by now I did not care. I was working for a major brick supplier company in the RTP area that most builders used in North Carolina and I was living a pretty comfortable lifestyle on my own, so I just let him go. I started partying hard on the weekends again and my promiscuous lifestyle came back into play hard. I was so wreck less with my decisions. I would drive out of town forty five minutes to an hour by myself to meet people in bars and strip clubs just to feed the hungry sexual spirit living inside of me. I was not concerned about home because I knew the kids were okay. My son would either be with his father that weekend and my daughter was watched by my sister and my little cousins, who basically owned my townhouse because I was never home or the kids would be home and have a bunch of company over because my house was the hangout spot for all ages.

There were times I would pick up someone and of course he thought he was picking me up and after we had sex, I would lay there and just cry because the void was still there. I would remember the first time I was touched when I was a little girl and convince myself that that was all I was good for. I felt like I did not exist if I did not have a man touching on me and degrading me in some way. Although I felt prettiest when I got the attention of men, I felt so ugly after because no one ever stayed for long.

Chapter Twelve
Christina's Spiral

Around Thanksgiving of the same year, keep in mind it is still 2003 and I just got married a couple of months prior, my husband and I decided to try it again. That December he brought me another car, a 2001 Ford Contour and we vowed to try to make our relationship work. Well, all was well until I had the rent money stolen from me. During this time, my husband had started using more than he was selling so the money was not like it used to be. Having to pay the money plus another month's rent right after he had just purchased me a car put a huge dent in our finances and an even bigger dent in our relationship. The night before New Year's Eve, December 30, 2003 I had just returned home from the hospital with the flu. I still had a temperature of one hundred and two degrees and it was looking like he was going to have to nurse me back to health for the biggest party night of the year. He was not even trying to hear that. I do not know what word I said that he let be a trigger for an argument but the last thing I remember him saying as he was walking out the door was that he was telling me Happy New Year then because he wouldn't see me when it came in. The door slam so hard behind him a picture fell off my wall.

By His Stripes

With every ounce of strength I could find, I went out the door minutes later and drove to my grandmother's house to call him. After hearing all the you should not be out of bed and you need to get back home, someone asked me where my husband was at. I told them that they asked something I too wanted to know and that is why I was getting ready to call him. What he said on the phone, I do not know. My head was spinning. I know he said he was not coming home. I left my grandmother's house in route to where I knew he was, but I should have been headed home. I ended up spinning out of control to avoid a deer and of course I was speeding. My car spun around four times on a small dark country back road.

I remember calling the name "Jesus" over and over again. A warm bright light filled my car and I came to a hard stop. What I did not know at that moment was how I stopped. I sat there shaking and crying wondering what to do next. With me being on a county back road, I could not see anything at all so I just sat there. I did not know where I was or what my car looked like. By the grace of God people started driving by. It seemed like slow motion as I watched car after car screech to a halt and passengers of all races jumped out and ran towards me. I could hear distantly people screaming in the background if I was okay. I think I was just looking at them because why were they talking to me... just get me out. By the time the ambulance pulled up, seeing as how they had to pass my grandmother's house to get to me some of my relatives had come down there to the wreckage site. I could hear the piercing screams of my family as I thought to myself that I was dead. I had to have been dead because why were people acting like that and why could they not hear me. Fire and rescue got there and cut me out of the front seat and it took six of them linking arms and two of them getting in the car to get me out. I could feel them passing me up a hill which was weird to me because I thought I was sitting straight up. By now, my husband was pulling up. He almost drove into a ditch I remember as he saw what it was that he saw. He got in the back of the ambulance with me and I could hear them saying words like "paralysis, popping sound, in and out of consciousness" as we drove to the closest hospital.

I later learned that my car ended up face down in between two trees down an embankment. I was two feet away from the pond and the car was totally destroyed. The whole trunk was mashed in and crumbled like a piece of balled up paper and the it was in the back seat. The driver's seat that I was sitting in had reclined all the way back and not only was it in the back seat but it was up under the trunk. I knew that it was nobody but God that kept me. I thought about how I could only say the name Jesus when I was wrecking and how that was a time in my life where cursing came naturally to me. In that moment profanity did not leave me lips. I truly feel like the angels reminded me to call on the only name that could help me in that moment.

By the grace of God, I walked away from the hospital that night but not after giving my family a scare. Two weeks later I was scheduled for surgery for a completely different situation. It is now January 2004 and I was facing an eviction because I no longer was receiving the housing assistance I had, my husband wasn't going to give me anymore money, and I wasn't working because I had just finished recovering from the flu and the wreck.

This is a time of darkness that had it been up to the devil, I would of totally lost my mind. I went from being the person everyone called on for help, the person that assisted close family and friends with paying their bills and keeping their lives in tact to having mine fall apart and no one to call on. Everyone that I could reach when I was on top of the world were now missing in action. My phone no longer was ringing and my calls were going unanswered. I had people telling me once again how much of a failure I was and my family in their disappointment did what they did best, they talked about me to whoever would listen. The whispers behind closed doors became the insults screamed loudly when they reached the ears of someone who did not mind telling me what they had heard. No one asked what happened to the job, it was just said that once again Christina lost a good job.

There were so many things that if someone had just shown me love, instead of judging me, that could have been handled differently. I am not crying over spilled milk now, I am just saying that from that, I learned that when someone is down, do not kick them. Find out from them what is going on and how you can help. We need to go back to the days were families stuck together no matter what and not pick and choose who to love and assist.

Within in this same time frame, I went into the hospital for a procedure called LEEP. It was to remove cancerous cells from cervix and it was supposed to be safe. Well, as you have already read, I had that if anything can go wrong it would go wrong with me. After the procedure they told me that I would have light bleeding for a couple of days and that would be it. That was on the 16th of January. By my birthday six days later, I was still bleeding and was extremely fatigued. I called the doctor and I guess because I was a Medicaid patient I was brushed off. During this time I knew I was going to have to move. I went into my son's room and laid on the floor on my face before God and just poured my heart out to Him. I apologized for all that I had done and told Him how I needed His help. I did not know what to do and if He did not mind, could He tell me. I got up off the floor waiting for something miraculous, but feeling better mentally all the same. I was still bleeding and went to lay down. I went to the emergency room and they looked at me and sent me home. They did not even want to touch me. I called my mom and she came and got me and took me to her house. She handled the move for me and enlisted one of my friends to help clean the townhouse and turn the keys back in. I was too physically week to finish what I had started with the packing and stuff but my mother took care of the rest for me. After laying around her house for a few days, on January 24th I could hardly get out of the bed to go to the bathroom. Every time I stood up, grapefruit sized blood clots would fall out of me at one time. I was turning white and could barely keep my eyes open. My mother grabbed some pads and towels and stuffed them down my pants and loaded me up in the car to go to the hospital.

By now, it had started snowing outside and it was not a light snow either. It was heavy and it was sticking. I remember the nervousness my mother had and how she was on the phone with one of her good friends who told her to come pick her up and she would go with us. Fifteen minutes later, when we got to her house, I had saturated the five pads, two thick towels, and sweat pants that I had on. I think her friend said something about the seriousness of the blood I was losing and it was then that I saw my mother cry. They helped me change into some more pants and gave me some more towels and got me to the hospital. Triage sent me straight to a room just from looking at me. I was pale. While in the back it was discovered that for my height and weight, I should have had approximately ten pints of blood in my body but when they checked I only had five. I had lost half of my blood mass.

They scheduled an emergency blood transfusion and my mother actually left to go get my husband because at the point together or not, we all felt he should be there. While the doctors were telling me what was going to happen next and the risks of receiving blood, the stubborn spirit reared it's head. I did not want it. They were telling me things like if the blood is contaminated it may not show up right now and it would be in me and a whole lot of other scary stuff. My mother asked them if she could just give me some of hers. That is that mother's love for you. She was willing to give up her own for me. They told her that was not going to be possible and that they needed to convince me to sign the papers. I was told that I literally had minutes to live. They came in and burn the vein that was bleeding but they told us it wasn't going to hold that long and that in fact, as soon as I stood again, the bleeding would return. It was to buy time. I called a couple of people that I knew that knew the words of prayer and I called a friend that had to have a transfusion when she gave birth to her first child. After half way hearing each person tell me to stop being scared I finally signed the papers or lack thereof, because also at this point I was losing my vision. My body was shutting down and I was being stubborn because of a disease that wasn't even guaranteed that could happen.

 I fell asleep during the first two pints that they put back in my body. I woke during the third round and was happy to see my husband sitting there. His phone rang and when he answered it, the person on the other line had a whole lot of questions about where he was, who he was with, and why he was there. He answered each question without a problem. When he got off the phone, I inquired who was he talking to that needed all that information. This joker starts yelling at me at how nosey I am and how he did not have to put up with it and he stormed out the hospital room. I laid there in disbelief, but what else could I do? He came back thirty minutes later to tell me that he was leaving. He ended up staying because he could not find anyone to come get him in the snow storm, but when I got out the hospital he did find his way home and left me at my parents house to recuperate by myself.

Once again, I wanted it to work with us so although sick, I drove the forty minutes to his house to try to talk to him. He would not open the door, he would not even acknowledge that I was out there. I was too weak to drive back to my parents so I balled up in a ball and went to sleep in the car. I guess his mother came out and saw me because she walked up to the car banging on the window about how stupid I was and for me to bring my dumb tail in the house. I followed him out of desperation and being tired. Although I did not have to be there, I wanted to.

When I was strong enough to get up I went back to my parents house and once again before long I was working and saving money. I found a job at a local real estate appointment setting company and joined a local gym which my best friend would come out to work out with me in the mornings before my shift was to start. I tried once again to work it out with my husband and at this point I did not realize just how bad his drug habit was. We hardly saw each other which to me was just fine, but the drugs had him paranoid that not only was everyone against him, but that I was his worst enemy. I should of paid attention to the signs that destruction was near but like before just to have a body in the bed with me and someone to share my life with, I did not notice. We started back clubbing again and I started looking for women to take on my wifely duties of sleeping with him so that I wouldn't have to. Funny thing is, while I was looking for someone to sleep with him, I was looking for someone else to satisfy my own sexual desires. Eventually we broke up yet again and I settled into a lifestyle of drugs, work, and alcohol to compensate for the pain I had on the inside of feeling like I was not accepted.

I started talking back to my daughter's father. He was always around but we usually flirted with each other from afar. His poor girlfriend caught havoc from me. I made sure she knew that I was in the picture and he was in my bed every chance that I got. It did not matter what I did though, she would not leave him alone. I finally figured out that although I was saying she had no self esteem to put up with a man that spent most of his nights with me on her car, I too was an emotionally wreck trying to convince her and myself that he and I had something. This went on for a couple of months before the partying caused me to lose yet another apartment and job.

The kids went to stay with family and once again I hit the streets. I started spending the night with friends and ended up with a friend that had I stayed, I would have been sucked back into the lifestyle of sniffing cocaine again. It just so happened that my ex and I got back together yet again and we go a trailer out in the country. This was when I discovered just how bad his habit had become. We had a triple wide three bedroom trailer and the only furniture we had was my daughter's bed, a dining room table, a washing machine and dryer, and a couch. And it stayed like that the whole time we were there. When I first moved in, I was so excited for what was to come. I was glad to once again be doing good and called all my sisters and some of my cousins over for a night of fun. We all stayed up the whole night and talked, danced, and just had a good time. A couple of weeks after that he and I were sleeping in separate rooms. Since we had no furniture he slept on the couch and I slept on a futon mattress in the third bedroom by myself. We lived like this for less than a month while I outwardly tried to give the appearance that I was okay.

Valentine's Day 2005 we decided to go out and we must have had a good time because the next morning I woke up next to him. It had been months since we had any kind of connection but the minute I woke up, I knew I was pregnant. I left the house that morning on his car under the pretense of coming back and stayed gone. When he finally figured out I was not coming back, he repossessed his vehicle and that was the end of that.

I was miserable. I was pregnant with a child that I did not want at that time. How was I going to bring another baby into the world and I was at such a low point. I looked on the internet for ways to cause miscarriages and I tried everything I read. I went to have an abortion not once but twice. I am still being billed to this day for both procedures. I went into a deep depression and was taken out of work around my sixth month of pregnancy. No one knew I was still carrying the child except my family. I literally went into hiding.

My belly did not start swelling until around the eighth month and even then depending on what I wore you could not tell I was pregnant. When doctors gave me my final due date I marked the day on my calendar with the words Spawn of Satan Birthday. One of my aunt's even offered to take my child in because I was considering adoption and everything. I did not want this man's baby. All of that changed on the day she was born. That October I gave birthday to a healthy baby girl who was literally born smiling. How could you not fall in love with someone who was so happy to be here. My hospital room was full of family when she came out and her birth story remains one of the funniest because of the fact there were like fifty people hiding in the bathroom waiting for her birth. I decided to keep my baby and called her father to come and meet her. He showed up for all of five minutes and laid no claim to our child. That was fine with me. I was used to him being absent at this point.

I moved back in with my parents and attempted to settle in on the path to getting myself back together. This visit was short lived, by December 26th we were out. For about a month I stayed with my daughter's grandmother and then eventually I moved in with my sister Tiffany and her baby boy. I asked her to give me at least two months to get my money back up and true to my word, I got a job and moved me and my girls into a townhouse on the other side of town. The brick company that I had worked at years before gave me my job back and I started once again trying to rebuild my life.

I still was not happy. My job was an hour commute from my home, my baby girl daycare was on one side of town and my oldest daughter had to get dropped off for school another twenty minutes outside of where we were. I was starting to feel the pressures of doing it all by myself. I was given time limits on when to pick my kids up and coming from the area I worked in, sometimes I did not meet the requirements. One morning, when my baby was about five months old, I prepared to take them to school so I could go to work and while we were leaving my lights got cut off. In a rush to take my baby to daycare, I failed to put her some formula in the bag. When I got to my job, an hour away, there was a message waiting for me to bring her some milk. I had enough gas in my car to get back home, but I didn't know what I was going to do about the trip back. When I got to the daycare with the milk, I was also informed that I owed money and until I paid it she would not be able to return. I gathered my baby and headed back to a dark house. While sitting there, I mustered up the strength to go get some help to get the lights back on. I went and picked my oldest daughter up early and we went back home. I do not even remember dinner that night. I put my baby in her crib and closed the door to her room. For the next fourteen hours I left her in there. She cried and her crying turned to screams but I would not open the door.

My seven year old was in her room and she had enough to occupy her that the crying did not really bother her. I climbed in my bed and I laid there. I just laid there. Finally I got up and went in and got my baby out of her bed. She was still breathing and sleeping but she really needed a bath. She smelled so bad and had feces all over her from her diaper not being changed for almost twenty four hours. I ran water in the bathtub and gave her a bath and a bottle. With tears in my eyes, I began to write good bye letters to my family. I apologized over and over again for what they were going to find, but I just couldn't take it anymore. I did not feel like I could call my mother or father, I felt alone, and I was in pain. I now know this was Post Traumatic Stress Disorder from having my baby, but at the time I had no clue what was wrong with me.

The moment I gathered the courage to take my life and the life of my kids, my sisters knocked at the door. All of them. God had sent them there and told them something was going on. My sister Tiffany like I mentioned earlier has always had the gift of discernment and she had called one of my aunts and told her I was going to need her to take the kids for a while. I never cried so hard in my life. Despite what I was getting ready to do, the Holy Spirit still intervened on my behalf and allowed me another chance at life to get my assignment right.

I moved out of the townhouse and into transitional housing for a while. Transitional housing is a program that is offered to families and families with children to live in housing where they do not have to pay rent but have to save at least sixty to seventy five percent of their income and receive it all at the end of their stay. My aunt had my kids and they were thriving in the environment with her and were doing good. I missed a lot of first with my baby, but she was safe. I started going to counseling and for a while, things were good.

My youngest baby's father and I decided to give it a try around that Thanksgiving, which was good for me because my time was up in transitional housing and I needed somewhere to go anyway. I moved in with him and his mother, son, and sister and tried to make it work. I would go pick my kids up from time to time to bring them down for a visit and all seemed to be okay for a while.

Well, what I forgot was he was still using drugs and when he got high, he got high. One night we both went out but he had caught a flat tire on his way home. I am guessing as he was driving home the slower he had to drive the madder he got. Something ignited when he laid eyes on me because he immediately jumped on me and started fighting me like a crazed man. It is like three in the morning and I was screaming for my life as he was choking and slamming me and pulling me around the yard by my braids. At one point the only thing I could do was position my body to make it hard for him to get me and until he ran out of breath, this is what we did. He ended up calling a friend to come get him, guess he was running from the police that he was afraid was going to come, but they never came. I went into the house and into the room we shared and I locked the door and placed the dresser in front of it and cried myself to sleep. A couple of hours later I went outside and saw my hair all over the yard. I looked like it had snowed black snow it was so much of it out there. I called a friend that had a truck and she came and got me and we packed all my stuff that we could get in one trip and got me out of there. Before I left, I cut up all his clothes and wrote on the left shoe that he was a woman beater of every pair of shoes he had. That was the last time we ever tried to make our relationship work. It was finally over for us two, but unfortunately not the end of my being in domestic relationships.

Chapter Thirteen
CHRISTINA'S SEARCH

A few months later I was back to talking to my oldest daughter's father and working again at a job I had previously held, but because of my work ethics, they took me back. It started off with me spending every weekend with him, but ended up with me and the girls moving in with him so that we could save money to get a house. He was dating the same girl he dated every other time he and I had gotten together, but eventually that ended because there was no way that was going to continue and I was living there.

For a while, playing house was fun and it was all good until I started seeing the women he was dealing with. It seemed like every time I turned around he was caught cheating. I would threaten to leave if that was what he wanted, he would beg me to stay and that would be the end of that. In my mind, since he was begging me to be there, that must have been good for something.

The first time he hit me we argued because he had one of his ex girlfriends call him to wake him up for work. I was laying right there and he really had another woman be his alarm clock. His excuse was the fact that he did not think I was coming home that night. Ok, that was all well and good, but you are a grown man and you had an alarm clock. So it is like six something in the morning and we fighting like two opponents from the UFC because of a phone call. He pulled out a lot of my hair too, something about them sorry men pulling hair. But that did not stop me from fighting back. He tried to take my car and leave me so he could go to work. But I had to go to work as well so we fought in the car the whole time he drove to his job. He even opened the door at one point and tried to push me out.

I went back to the house got my children ready for daycare and school, dropped them off, and went to work. I confided in the girl who sat in the cubicle next to me what happened and ended up talking to her a lot of what was going on with my home life. The kids and I went to spend the night at my parents house and I had intended on telling them once again that I wanted to come home, but before I could, I was asked when were we going home and I kept quiet. I went back and stayed with him longer and the fighting got worse. The more he acted out the more I did too. The more he cheated, the more I cheated. It did not help that his father was an alcoholic and at his drunkest moments he walked through the house cursing and yelling about killing his ex wife and her new husband. It was his fault she had left him, but he blamed everyone else but himself. Living in that house was a very miserable time, but it was better than going here and there and everywhere with my kids in tow. One of my cousins did not live too far away and I would go to her house and drink my cares away and complain about a man that I was not going to leave.

By His Stripes

I ended up getting pregnant by him and I knew that I could not bring a baby into that house. I just couldn't. Off to the abortion clinic I went. It was a two day process since I was so far along. The first day they gave me a pill that stopped the baby's heartbeat and the second day they would actually extract the fetus from my stomach. I would of only had approximately ten maybe ten and half weeks left. I was really far along. But I did not want a baby. Night one was horrible. As time wore on I could feel the baby inside of me fighting for his life. (I later learned it was a boy). I cried and tried to stay busy as I could feel the struggle for life taking place inside of me. I kept apologizing to my baby and made promises that I had no right to make. He went out with his friends because he could not stand to deal with it. He said since it was my decision to kill his baby, I would have to go through it alone. The next morning I got dropped off at the clinic and when the baby was removed one of the nurses exclaimed how big he was. She was immediately removed from the room but the damage had been done.

When he and I started back having sex again, I was careful to make sure we had plenty of condoms available. Imagine my surprise when I ended up pregnant again. He told me that he had poked holes in the condoms before we used them because he knew if I was pregnant I would stay. There was no way I was going to kill this baby, I still was not over the last one. I called my sister and told her that I was yet again with child. This would be my fourth one. I opted not to tell anyone. But they would all find out soon enough.

We ended up moving out of his father's house into a house across town. For a while we were okay. We were not fighting and he was happy because I was giving him another baby. One of my cousins would come by and we would sit on the porch and drink a glass of red wine and just talk everyday.

One night, just to get out we went to the club with some friends. As usual, some of my sisters were over, which was not unusual and they were planning on spending the night. On this particular night, my then boyfriend had went out as well and he got high and drunk as well. It was later told to me that when the cocaine ran out and he did not have anything else to sniff that he started crushing up pills from the medicine cabinet of the bathroom at the house they were at. No one thought the drugs was doing anything to him and took him home. I received a phone call from one of my sisters telling me that he came home and put them all out. She said that he had cursed them out and even went to get his sister from next door to help him reiterate his case of wanting them gone. When I got home, I went to check on the girls and saw that his niece was still there. This made me mad. How he put my family out but let his stay? So I woke her up and told her to get out too. Then I started with him. I went and woke him up, yelling and cursing and pushing on him to shake him awake. Well, he did wake up, but not the way I anticipated. He immediately began punching me like never before. He hit me so hard that although I was standing straight up, I flipped over backwards and landed back on my feet. It was something like in the movies. He punched and kicked me and I remember shielding my stomach. Although he was only swinging at my face and each time his fist impacted it burned I could only think about the unborn baby in my stomach. After he got tired of hitting me, he grabbed his phone, called his dad to come get him and started grabbing clothes. I thought he had left at one point and I locked the door he went out of. Well, he wasn't and when he realized he could not get back in, he kicked a hole in the door and forced his way back in.

Feeling like there was no one to call, I climbed into the bed and cried myself to sleep. The next morning, the cousin I had went out with called to say she was coming to get her stuff from the night before. Although I told her everything, I did not tell her what happened. I know I answered the phone and I could barely talk. I just mumbled to her the door would be open and I laid back down. I could not feel my face. I finally went to the bathroom and looked in the mirror. The creature that looked back at me was hideous. I was totally disfigured. Between the swelling and the shifted cheekbones, I have no idea how to describe the mess that he left me with. I know I called him. Part of me wanted to see if he remembered what he did to me, part of me felt he knew what he was doing. He came over and when he saw me the tears started. He went and got his sister who had went to school for a while for nursing and when she came back she cried. She apologized for what her brother did to me and told me he needed to be locked up. I told him he needed to keep the kids because I was going to the hospital. His first response was that he would but it was what he said next that would change the relationships with me and my family for years to come. He asked me what would I tell them happened to me. He wanted to know how I would explain the beating and who would I say gave it to me. I made up a story. It makes no sense even now but from what I can remember, I said I was walking on the train tracks and someone tried to rape me and I fought them off. At least that is what I think I said.

I called my sister Veronica and told her to come to the hospital. I asked her to keep it to herself. Anyone that knows her knows she can't hold her breath, let alone a secret. She did not come alone and she actually got there with my other sister at the same time as my boyfriend and his father. It did not take long for the word to get out that I was in there. I had never seen my grandfather cry. My granddaddy is a strong man and for him to break down when he walked into the room killed me. It took all I had not to point to the corner of the room and say he did it, but at this point there was a lot of family there and the riot would have been ugly. It was when the doctor announced in front of everyone that they were sending me to the OB/GYN section of the hospital to monitor the baby that everyone found out I was six months pregnant.

Can you believe after all of this I still wanted to be with this man? I wanted to believe that the incident had changed him and that we could make it work for the sake of the children. Plus, I did not want to go home. A couple of days later my mom came to my house with what seemed like every cop in town, begging me to press charges. She held my hand and told me that I did not have to go through that and I could always come home no matter what, but I just couldn't. My Pastor told me I had a "I just don't want her to have him spirit". I did not want to lose him to his ex that I fought so hard to take him from. Doctors had said they would have to perform surgery on my face after I gave birth to repair the damage, but the compassionate loving God that I know today decided to heal my body and restore my face to the one that He gave me.

We moved again, this time deeper into the country, but because people knew deep down inside he was the one that did it to me, my family did not come over like they had before. No one wanted to be around him. But I loved him so I stayed.

That September I gave birth to a feisty ready for anything little girl. After her birth, I learned that he had started using drugs again. I was often asked did I not know, and truthfully I did not. I thought the experience of disfiguring me had changed him. I had no issues from him. He went to work and he came home. He had friends over but he was always home at night. His paycheck came straight to me and he was really doing everything he could to make me happy.

When I found out that he was using again our fights started back up. We had a gun for protection since there were a lot of break ins in our area. One day we were fighting and I grabbed the gun. I will admit I grabbed it first but the tables turned real quick. My oldest two girls were not home from school yet and my five month old was laying in her bassinet when we began rumbling all over our trailer. I can't tell you what the fight was about, but it turned serious real quick. I lost the gun when he picked me up and smashed me through the wall. After peeling myself out of the hole, I went and grabbed the bassinet hoping he would see the baby being tossed and he would stop. He did stop, but not before picking up the gun. We fought to gain control of the gun which was off safety and my baby was laying right there. No one broke us up, we just stopped. He ended up leaving to go call his father to come get him and as usual I cried myself to sleep.

That was on a Friday. That Sunday, I went to church and told my leaders what happened. After explaining to me how once this point of escalation is reached death is likely time to follow I made it my business to let it go. It was a hard decision to make but I did call the police and I pressed charges. He and I broke up obviously and we have never rekindled our relationship.

Three months after that, my lease was up where we lived and although I did not want to, I moved home. During this time, my sister had left her husband and she was living home as well. With all of us being in the same house, God laid it on the hearts of my parents to let us get the house and for them to downsize to an apartment to help all of us get ourselves together. I had already given my life to Christ but was not trying to seriously walk in deliverance until I got out of the country town I was living in.

I went back to work and devoted my time to healing and moving forward. Despite of all we went through, I still found myself having moments of missing the girls' dad, and he was the only man I would cheat on God for, but with prayer and fasting he was being removed from my system. I knew that my kids only had me to depend on and that their wellbeing would be dependent on me. I was working two jobs just to provide and pay for daycare. Actually, my second job, I never saw one cent from. It was all just to pay for daycare. I would leave my fulltime job during the day and go work at night just to make sure that while working the kids had somewhere to go. I was so tired during this time, but happy at the same time because I was providing for my children and I was just in a better space. I still could not get consistent help with them, but at least now I was not angry about it. I just knew that I had to do what I had to do, no matter how much I hated it.

My best friend invited me on a trip to Vegas about seven months later and it was when I returned that all hell broke loose once again in my life. My car broke down, I was laid off from my job, and I lost my daycare. This was very hard to take in because at this point in my life I am like God, what is it.

I could not understand why I was at this place again but this time, instead of running away, I planted my feet firmly in the word and decided to ask God what was the lesson I needed to learn. I knew that there was something that would come out of this. My sisters and I talked and we decided that we would figure it out by any means necessary. I looked for work, but could find none. I started focusing on my gift basket business again, and although it did not pay the rent, it was enough to help us with just what we needed. Don't get me wrong, that did not mean it was all sweet. The enemy stayed in my ear and he even used close friends to remind me of the low that I had once again hit. I was reminded that although I still talked about being blessed, all people could see was what I did not have. Although there was a stable roof over the head of my children and I, all people saw was I was living in a house with all my sisters. Things like that did eat at me for a while, but it also helped me to build my faith in God even more. Man did not understand how I was still going on as if I did not have a care in the world, although I did not. Here I am living my life for Christ, I go to church every Sunday, and I had made a lot of changes. 2010 was full of losing stuff it seemed like. My sisters and I banded together though and made it work. We grew closer with each other than ever before. Things started turning around for me that November when a church gave me a car. That blessing came right on time for me seeing as how having kids you need transportation. As the season began to change and the temperature started dropping outside, my sisters and I did not have enough money to turn the heat on in the house. For a couple of weeks we endured the cold and all busted our butts to get the deposit needed to put heat in the house. We still went to church and praised God as if there were no issues in our lives.

Flash forward a couple of months my parents decided that they were going to move back home and allow two of my sisters and my two nephews to take over the apartment they were renting. I still had not found a job and my only contribution was the child support check I received every month which was enough to supply the needs of my children and myself. My dad would constantly ask me what was I doing, what was I going to do, and what were my plans. I did not have any answers for him because during that time, I was asking God the exact same things. I wanted to know when was my breakthrough coming and how long did I have to live like that. I would tell my dad of how I was trusting God for the change and that all I had to answer Him with was my faith. Funny how faith is an answer that works when it is someone else. But I truly did have nothing but faith that God was doing something different this time and that He was preparing me to be ready for it when it came.

That summer I received a prophecy that by the end of 2011 I would not be living in my parents house. There was some other things said to me, but that really stood out to me. Now we all have our expectations of how God is going to do something in our lives and when it happens we forget that He is keeping His promise if it does not happen the way we anticipate. That November my mother and I got into one of our normal arguments and she decided she wanted everybody out the house and everybody that had a key had to give it back. I remember my sister Veronica saying well what did I do? We laugh about it now, but it was not a laughing matter then. Usually when that situation happens, I go running back to the arms of some man that can put me up until I can stand on my own. To add insult to injury, my car broke down the very next week. Out of all things that could go wrong, I had a blown head gasket. Surely this would make me breakdown I could imagine the devil thought. But this time was different, I was still walking with God and my relationship with Him had actually grown stronger. The week of Thanksgiving, my children and I moved into a shelter. At first, it was the hardest thing to do and I did not want to talk about it. God reminded me that He sent the Woman of God to tell me I would not be in my parent's house by the end of the year. Well, He kept His word. I was not there. My faith was tested over the course of the next few months as we lived in the program that I was trusting we were in for a reason. I knew that no matter what, the God I served would not take me there to leave me there.

I vowed to learn everything it was he would have for me to learn. I praised Him despite of the fact that I just did not feel like it. I praised Him through the tears of not having a real home for the holiday season. I praised Him because each week He showed me that He had me. He had complete strangers coming up to me placing money in my hand. He allowed me the time I did not have before to spend with Him and only Him. When my kids would go to sleep at night, I would sneak off to the sanctuary of the church we were staying at and just rejoice and marvel in His goodness. I left the program with more than I had when I was going in, but most importantly I developed a walk on water faith. God showed me who I was and then He showed me who He made me to be.

He had already told me to begin writing this book and for the longest time I procrastinated. After I procrastinated I started trying to figure out how it was going to be published. See, did you catch what was wrong with that statement? I was trying to figure stuff out and that is not what God told me to do. He told me to write. He told me to tell where I was so people could see where He is taking me. My deliverance of the demons that tormented me was not an easy one and it did not happen quickly because I was not willing to let go. I wanted to be made whole long enough to feel good. But then God started showing me the lives attached to my testimony that could not change until I surrendered to Him. He showed me that He gifted us all to gift others. I have always had a way with people and God knew that when He created me. He knew that my passions about something would ignite the passion in the one I was sharing it with. I just had to let go and let Him.

Chapter Fourteen
CHRISTINA'S REDEMPTION

What I gained from that experience is more than I can possibly think to ask for. Actually, anyone in their right mind, would not ask for the experiences. If we could gain the things that God has given me without going through the trials to get it, I know I would be the first in line for that option.

Being back on my own, I have a new found appreciation for it. I also know that if it had not been for the Lord, who was truly on my side, none of this would be happening. My kids and I moved into our home with the clothes on our backs. Within months, God had furnished our whole house, many of the items brand new, by touching people to just give to us and to sow into our lives. I heard a sermon that the scripture text came from the Book of Joel. It talked about how God promises to restore all that was taken and destroyed. The sermon reminded me of what God does for those that remain faithful. The blessings that He has given to me, I can only explain by saying that God does not promise something and not fulfill it.

I truly have committed my life to not only pleasing Him, but being used by Him, by any means necessary. I also agreed to give myself away to Him totally, as the song worshiper William

McDowell sings. I know that in order for Him to do in me what He has called to be done, I had to go through the pit and the process therein. I know that these things were for His glory and He will be glorified because of the sacrifice.

I actually called the men in this book and asked them to forgive me. This may sound strange to some, but I was wrong to hold grudges against them walking with God who had forgiven me. I asked them to forgive me for not forgiving them. I apologized for my part in our dysfunctional relationships.

I also asked God to reveal the spirits in me that were not like Him that was hindering me from walking in my full deliverance. Although my Pastor and Elder prayed over me and helped me to ask for deliverance of some, there were some underlining issues that I learned I had the authority through Christ to demand on my own to leave me. Some of these spirits had been residing in me since I was a little girl and up until my adult life, I did not know how to call them out until God revealed their names to me.

The spirit of bitterness was there and with it was hatred, unforgiveness, and retaliation. There are a lot of parts of my story that God did not have me to write about, but I was good at getting back at people. I could carry grudges for a long time and even when it seemed like I was okay with a person, I was secretly concocting ways to pay them back for something they had done to me.

I also struggled with the spirit of rebellion. I was very disobedient as a child and when I got older it developed into stubbornness. If I did not want to do something, I just did not do it. Through my drug use and my binge drinking, the spirit of destruction and addiction ran rampart inside of me. Because of the unworthy feelings I had towards my self and the fear of rejection which also was something I needed deliverance from, I sought for comfort in ways that led to destroying my body.

Although doctors said that I was another case of bipolar disorder, God showed me that the spirit of withdrawal and unreality was in me. I would go on spending binges like I had the money and when I came off that emotional high I had to deal with the reality of life.

Going back to my drug use, the spirit of escape is one that also needed to be called out and placed into submission to the blood of Jesus. I would use them to take me away from what it was I was going through at the moment. I would also use them to help give me the courage to do some of the things that I did that ordinarily, I would not have done.

From the first time I was touched by that grown man when I was a little girl to each time I let a man use my body for his own gratification, the spirit of heaviness was right there to feed off of all of it. I was so disgusted with myself. I hated what I was doing and what was being done to me, but at the same time I felt like it had to be done.

It was only when I got into the word of God and started truly applying it to my life that the healing actually began. Talking about what I had been through and how God kept me through it all also helped. The more I told and tell my story the more the spirit of shame has to find somewhere else to reside. ***The very first scripture that I started to embrace was Jeremiah 29:11, "For I know the plans I have for you" declares the LORD, "plans to prosper you and not to harm you, plans to give you hope and a future."*** This one helped me to know that what I had chosen for myself was not what He had chosen for me. When I was longing for more of Him and wanting to be closer to Him but feeling unworthy to even ask, ***Psalm 119:169-176 helped me. It reads " May my cry come before you, Oh Lord, give me understanding according to your word. May my supplication come before you; deliver me according to your promise. May my lips overflow with praise, for you teach me your decrees. May my tongue sing your word, for all your commandments are righteous. May your hand be ready to help me, for I have chosen your precepts. I long for your salvation, Oh Lord, and your law is my delight. Let me live that I may praise you, and may your laws sustain me. I have strayed like a lost sheep. Seek your servant, for I have not forgotten your commands."*** The things He told me when I would tell Him of how dirty I was and I lived such a sinful life and I would ask Him what could He possibly do with me, He told me to read ***Genesis 50:20. "You intended to harm me, but God intended it for good to accomplish what is now being done, the saving of many lives."*** He reminded me that not everything that happens to us is good and some of the stuff we bring on ourselves, but devoting our lives to Him, He has the power and authority to rewrite the ending. He let me know that even my bad stuff can still be worked to glorify Him. He sent me to read **Romans 8:28-30, *"And we know that in all things God works for the good of those who love Him, who have been called according to His purpose. For those God foreknew, He also predestined to be formed to the likeness of His son, that he might be the firstborn among many brothers. And those He predestined, He also called; those He called, He also justified; those He justified, He also glorified." And last but not least, while on my road to healing and deliverance He reminded me of Isaiah 53:5, " But He was wounded for our transgressions, He was bruised for our iniquities: the chastisement of our peace was upon Him; and with HIS STRIPES WE ARE HEALED.***

Today God has placed my kids and I in our own home, I am walking in the things He has called me to walk in, one of which is a ministry birthed by my Pastor entitled Silent Sins in the Church. It is a ministry dedicated to the education of and healing of victims of domestic violence and sexual assault and every chance I get I talk about the goodness of my Jesus.

May each chapter you read in this book be a reminder of the beating that Jesus took for us all and the healing that lies in wait for us from any situation we may have been through.

EPILOUGE
AUTHOR'S REFLECTIONS

So there you have it. You know some pretty deep details about me. But that is not where the story ends. Actually my story does not end until the day I die or the day Jesus returns for His church, whichever one happens first.

I now can talk to you about how I now can face all my trials and know that it will be okay because I am living in forgiveness through Jesus Christ.

I am no longer the same girl that holds in mistakes and things that will have me in a position to be judged because I am afraid of what people may think. When I fall, I say I fell. Psalm 37:24 teaches us that if we will try to do His will, God will uphold us with His right hand. My Pastor taught me that God does majestic things with His right hand. His right hand is the side where Jesus is seated. He tells us of His own hand laying out the foundations of the earth and how it was His right hand that spread out the heavens. (Isaiah 48:13) So you see, being upheld by the right hand of God is pretty important.

I was able to witness God's right hand at work a couple of years ago when my daughter, who was just two years old at the time, fell out the car while I was driving. I was in such a rush to drop them off that I did not secure her car seat in the car.

By His Stripes

Thankfully, she was strapped into the seat but had I been more responsible I could have avoided a lot of heartache. I later called the incident "Lesson learned a Blessing Earned". We were sitting at a stop light when I made a right turn on red and heard my other daughter scream out. I turned around to see what she was yelling for when I saw the back passenger side of the car door open and my baby's car seat falling out. I did not even place the car in park when I removed my own seatbelt and jumped out of the car, leaving my five year old in a moving car by herself. There was an eighteen wheeler behind us but by nothing but the grace of God it was moving extremely slow. Also there was a Good Samaritan on the side of the road who jumped in my car to place it in park during the time that I had jumped out of the car to grab my baby. When her car seat came to a stop, I grabbed her seat and ran crying back to my car looking for the nearest medical attention. Nearly half of her face was rubbed raw down to the white meat, it wasn't even bleeding anymore. Upon her release from the hospital she was given a clean bill of health (no broken bones) and I was not charged with neglect. How favorable was that? Granted it could have been avoided, but like my grandfather always says, it also could have gone another way. I told my story to remind parents to slow down. There is nowhere that is so important that a moment cannot be taken to secure our children in cars. I was hard on myself for a while after that, but God was still good, healing her face in less than two week's time. To this day.

Telling that story reminds me of another reason this book was written. We are often times our worse critic. We are so hard on ourselves we miss the moments where God is telling us to come to Him and allow Him to heal and forgive us. We count ourselves out for the count as if we have every right to do so. We basically tells the Creator, do not make a fuss with me, I am not worth it. We in a sense tell Him that we are not worthy of His love and Jesus dying on the cross for our sins was a waste of time.

Who are we to do this? This was another hard lesson that I had to learn. Something I have learned in the past couple of years, when God tells us to do something, it will not always make sense. We just think we know it all and the logic behind the ludicrous request is weighed in our minds with what makes sense taking precedence over what the Lord says. Before I go into further detail with this, I must first show you an example of this in God's word. Yes, the Bible is truly a blueprint for everything that we go through in life.

In Luke Chapter 5, there is story of when Jesus finished a sermon and asked the fishermen if they had caught anything. They had been fishing all day and night and yet to catch one fish. Jesus told them to cast their nets to the other side of the boat. Now you can imagine that this idea was just crazy to them. They had been fishing all night long and not only that, but they were professionals in their field. If there was anyone that knew fishing it was Peter, James, John, and Andrew. It was Simon (Peter) who answered that since you say it will work, we will try it. This must have taken great faith on his part and his partners. The word lets us know that after doing so, their nets became so full of fish that they began to break and they had to have the other boats pulled in to help them lift them all. It is safe to say that because of their obedience and trying something that they had never tried before they were blessed abundantly in a way that would not have come just from fishing the same old way. Back to my children and I moving into the shelter. I had never gone into one before. There was usually a relative to go stay with to get on our feet or a friend's house to crash at. But this time, I felt lead to try something different. Although a shelter is the last place I wanted to be, I kept hearing the Lord ask me if I trusted Him. So that Sunday before Thanksgiving my kids and I moved in. We casted our nets to the other side. Almost immediately we were blessed with a catch. That first week we received so much stuff I was overwhelmed with the thought of where to put it all. The church we were staying at opened the doors to the clothing ministry for myself and the other families there and allowed us to just have our pick at the items donated throughout the months. There were people coming up to me and just placing money in my hand. They would tell me they were not sure why, but they just wanted to bless me with something. Again, this was just the first week and we were there for three months. Every week was like this. Not only that, but with us staying in churches, when the midnight hour came, I would sneak off to the sanctuary of the church we were staying at and just lay on my face at the altar before God and sing songs of worship and praise and just tell Him how good I still thought He was. I knew that God did not bring us there to leave us there. I did not know how long the journey would be, but I learned how to trust Him. My kids and I were blessed that each week we had our own room with four beds in it for the each of us. We had just what we needed for where we were at the time. This helped ease my mind as well as I had already mentally prepared myself for the shelter images I had already seen on television. During this season in my life, just as Jesus told Simon to not be afraid, He instructed me also not to fear because God was still in control.

Another hard lesson that I had to learn and I am still learning as I grow was one of forgiveness. I had to learn how to give it and how to go on if I did not receive it. I had to learn to apologize over and over again and I also had to learn how not to have ill feelings toward anyone that I felt had wronged me that just refused to apologize. As a matter of fact, as I am writing this, I laugh at myself even now because of the stubbornness I exuded when I just refused to try reestablish a relationship with someone that just wouldn't accept my offer. God was telling me to try again and I was just like nope. Yea, I was brave. I told God I could not do it. I had a serious tantrum because I thought it was not fair that I had to reach out to someone that hurt me. "What sense does that make?" I would say. "Why do I have to be the one?" I asked over again to what seemed like deaf ears. I was like Peter, once again, when He asked Jesus how many times he had to keep forgiving the one that hurt him. (Matthew 18:21-22) I remember talking to my Pastor and telling her to pray for me because I was yet to walk in obedience with that. It was later that I learned I could not keep track of someone else's wrongdoings and I did not want God to keep track of mine. I also learned that I was holding back my own blessings by not doing what the Lord said. It was one night sitting on the computer when I heard the Holy Spirit say to me in a stern voice, "Oh you just not were going to do it?" It was something about how He said it that made me realize how serious it was. I was stunting my own growth because of something that I did not have control over. My brothers and sisters let me tell you. There is nothing more humbling than going to someone that wronged you but you ask them to forgive you. But in order for us to receive the fullness of God's forgiveness, we must be willing to forgive others. There were many people that were close to me that broke my heart because of the writing of this book. They had not read it yet, nor had they asked me about it. They just felt that I had nothing I could possibly write about and some even felt I was looking for a get rich quick way of things. Let me tell you, I had to not only forgive them but I had to trust that God would do what He said

He would do through this book and just let Him fight the battle for me. It was heartbreaking to hear though some of the things that were said. I mean, after all I had been through, to see the woman that I am today that stands in my right frame of mind, how could one not want me to share my story. It also hurt because I am putting myself out there. Although God did not release me to tell you everything I experienced and did the things He did tell me to write about truly stripped me of any covering I may have been hiding behind. This book bears my naked soul and scars to all to see, read, and judge and there is nowhere for me to go hide. But in it all, I trust God. He said He would use my story to heal the people. I believe Him. He said He would use my mistakes to give a voice to His people and I truly believe that.

Before I Go

So with all that I have experienced, I want to leave you with this thought. What is it that I am holding that I may need to be healed from? What is keeping me from serving God fully and wholeheartedly? Am I really giving Him my all or just what I want to acknowledge? The things that I talked about in this book, the only reason I was able to be healed from them was because I took the power the shame of them had over me. To be healed is to be mended, to be cured, made whole, and to be returned to the original state. Once I was able to forgive those that hurt me, my heart was able to be mended. Once I let go of the shame only then was I able to be cured from the sickness that doctors labeled as being bipolar disorder. When I allowed God to reveal the true me as He sees me to me, then was I able to be made whole. I was able to be used by Him. You don't have to just go around exposing all your dirty laundry to world. But you do have to seek God's face and do what it is that He requires of you. All He asks is for a heart that will repent. He tells us to come to Him with our broken hearts and He promises to heal them. (Psalm 147:3) Anytime God speaks you can count on that as a promise. God is not like us that He speaks just to hear Himself speaking. Just a Word from Him activated in our lives through our faith makes us whole. (Luke 18:42) And last but not least, again I mention the importance of forgiving and lifting up each other. Although the death and resurrection of Christ opened the door for us to go to God directly for our forgiveness, it is still pertinent to go to our brothers and sisters as well. If we have sinned against someone , we are required to go to them to ask for forgiveness. If we have affected the Body of Christ in any way, we are to apologize to the church. There is no way around it. If we struggle with something or we have struggled with something, we should confess that sin so that we are able to be supportive to one another. (James 5:16)

As I leave you with my confessions, just know that He brought me through it so you can have a modern day example of the fact that He is still a Living God. The same God you read about that parted the Red Sea lives. The power and authority He gave Jesus to get up out of His grave on the third day after His crucifixion, is the same power and authority He gives to believers to battle any and every trial that we face.

ACKNOWLEDGMENTS

First and foremost I have to thank God. I never knew my worth until I looked at myself through the spiritual eyes of my Heavenly Father. I am thankful that salvation is available for us ALL and I am thankful for Jesus dying on the cross for me to have a chance to partake of it.

To my mother and father. Thank you. I love you both very much and I pray that as I grow you can see the woman that I am daily becoming and your hearts swell from being proud of the child you birthed. Because of you, and although you hate it sometimes, I learned how to be outspoken. I learned how to pump my own gas and change a tire. I learned how to make it happen by any means necessary. I know that we don't always see eye to eye, but I learned that no matter what, you should provide for your family. You taught me how to cook and how to clean the mess out of a house...... lol...... just not yours. I thank you for being there even when it was hard for you to do so. You watched me make bad decisions one after the other and when you were told to give up and walk away, you didn't. Thank you.

My firstborn, Christopher. I love you more than I think you will ever know. If I could turn back the hands of time, I don't know what more I could have done differently except for more time. I wish I knew then what I know now, but I am thankful for the opportunity yet and still to just have you in my life. You keep me on my toes and like myself, I never know what you are going to say, but I am so proud of you. You are turning out to be an awesome young man and when the day comes; your wife is going to truly be blessed to have you as her husband. I thank God for our own healing that He allowed us to go through with our relationship. Thank you for your forgiveness. It is amazing how much I have learned from you. (when you know what you are talking about…lol)

Nikia, my oldest daughter. You make me laugh even when you don't mean to. You have been through the most with me and in this book; you were there for a lot of the journey. You were born into chaos but you still found the beauty in it. Thank you for loving me flaws and all. Thank you for standing by me as I should have been the one standing for you. I love you so much. Looking at you now, I see so much of me in your physical attributes but I see so much strength I did not have at your age. I am proud that you are choosing to do things differently. I am proud of you for wanting to break the chain. I love seeing you seek more of God being a part of your everyday life. Contrary to what you think and say, you are a fighter. You could have given up a long time ago, but you did not. Keep pushing to birth the greatness in you!

Kai'anna, you are truly a gift from heaven. Why God chose me I still don't know. I just know that your life is significant and it truly matters. In my darkest hour, I did not recognize that, but I am so glad that God said yes when the devil tried to say no. Your dance inspires me to keep moving, your song reminds me to sing not for the listener but for my creator, and your softness reminds me it is okay to be fragile sometimes. I love you so much my little model. You praise as if you know what it took for you to get here and I know that although you are young, God is well pleased with you. I know we have yet to see what is in store for you, but I know with God's hand on it, it is going to be amazing!

Layla. Layla. Layla. Layla. My youngest child but age truly is just a number. You are the most technical child I know. You bring out so much in me. I have to stay on my toes with you. I love that although stubborn you are independent. Those traits will come in handy later... hold on to them. You are another that makes me laugh and like your big brother, I never know what you are going to say. Thank you for daily reminding me that Jesus kept me and to be so young, your worship inspires me to worship Him more. I love you Little Girl....

To my four queens, my best best friends, my sisters: Tiffany, Linda, Veronica, and Kayla. I can't even give you all an individual paragraph because honestly the love I have for you and the words to express it would turn into another book. We fight, we argue, we make up, we pray but most of all we are there for each other. Even when I feel the world is against me, I know I have you. Even when I am wrong and you don't mind telling me so, I know I have you. When I don't have a dollar to my name and when I have what seems like more than I need, I know I have you. So many times there have been some that came and left but you have always been consistent. People have often said they can't believe how close we all are, it has to be tiring. But it is not. We know when one is sick, we know the pain one feels and we also know when someone is in labor because we all feel it. When it felt like the weight of the world was on my chest it is then my phone rings and it is one of you calling to see what is going on. I love how in sync we are and how much we hate it all at the same time. The journey to publishing this book was beyond painful but you were right there to cry and laugh with me. THANK YOU. There is so much more that I could say, but you already know so I won't. My honorary sister, Miracle.... I will forever remember you throwing yourself in the line of fire for me. I do not think that memory will ever leave. That is love, you are love, and I love you! To my sister, Lina, your secrets are always safe with me as I know mine are with you. (the ones God did not have me to share)

To my brother in laws, Greg and Lamar... wait did I just mention two of you? Well, Lamar it is only a matter of time. But I thank God for the both of you. The love you have for my sisters is enough to make me love you but you being there for me and my kids is added icing on the cake. I love y'all. Thank you for being there and for pushing me forward.

To my spiritual parents, the leaders of TrueWay Apostolic Church where I attend, Pastor Gwendolyn and Elder Jeremiah Scott. From the first day in your congregation six years ago until now you have embraced me and big two of my biggest cheerleaders. When I felt like giving up you made me question why and for what to recognize the ludacrisy of it all on my own. Through you I learned how to face my battles and not to run away from them. I learned how to read the Word for myself and that it truly does apply to my life. When I finally decided abusive relationships were not a part of my destiny, it was from the words you spoke in your office. You got to know me and taught me to know me as God knows me. Even when outsiders tried to convince you of who I was, you only saw me for God said I would be. Thank you for being my "Abigails". You spoke life into me when the world spoke death. You disciplined as your own (contrary to what people think... I caught and still catch it from yall) and loved me the same. On the journey to the calling that God has ordained for my life, I am thankful that you are the sub-shepherds he appointed to guide me there. You are so humble and I learned humility through you. If it had not been for the teaching that I received from the both of you, I would not have been prepared for what God is doing now. How else can I say it but just, THANK YOU?

By His Stripes

To my church family. I know you all are some of the first to read this book.. some of the first to sow seeds into this book, and some of the main ones praying for me. Thank you and I love you all those here and the ones on the way. #coreforlife, Minister Tate, we are truly two of kind. Who would of thought? Greater is coming though! Brother Frank, keep pushing those walls. Just as they marched around Jericho and brought them down, so is your push. Prophetess, all I can say is, soon, very soon. To the Mothers of the church, thank you for your wisdom and for showing me what it looks like to be kept a mighty long time. To my choir family, Voices of Victory… I so love making a joyful noise with you all. To all my babies singing in Youth in Praise and stepping with Kingdom's Treasures, I am so proud of you all.

To my entire Living Waters Church Family, I love you all and I thank you so much for your prayers and your support. To Apostle Blue, Pastor Blue, Minister Cornelia Malloy, Elderess Cheryl Dudley, Minister Kalmakeisha McQueen, Minister Takaisha Elliot, and Minister Dana McDougan, thank you all for the prayers, phone calls, hugs, and covering on the battlefield. I love you all so so much and I thank God for the covenant between our churches.

Bishop Gearld Belcher and the Scotts Grove Church Family. Thank you so much for your prayers and just speaking a Word in the right time in my life. Bishop, you motivate me to keep writing what God gives me even when it does not make sense and for that I say THANK YOU!

Pastor Kim Hall and Task Ministries, I love you so much. Together we will continue breaking the silence and ministering to God's people. Can you say "Lord, have mercy?"

My church family at Church of God of Prophecy, State Street Raleigh, NC. You taught me enough and laid enough foundation in me that when I was old enough and at my ropes end, I knew to seek God's face. Thank you. I will not dare try to shout you out individually because I know I would miss somebody. But just know I love you all and cherish all my memories with you. I will never and I mean will never forget my Youth Outreach Choir family days. Talk about gifted!!!!!

Line Upon Line Precept Upon Precept International Ministries, Sr. Pastor Nannette Conover and Associate Pastor Dorothy Easton thank you for your prayers and encouragement. You both as well as the church family always push me to seek God more every time we are together. I love you all. Can't wait to see what God does with our kingdom connection.

To my bestie, Crystal, CAN YOU BELIEVE IT? As I look at what God is doing in my life and yours as well, I can't help but to remember when. I know we never saw the doors actually being opened that He has opened for us but He did it. Thank you for being you. You told me what I needed to hear and not what I wanted to hear on numerous of occasions. Thank you for being friend enough to check me when I was wrong and encourage me when I was right. Thank you for pushing me when I stopped moving. Thank you for sharing your dream with me and inspiring me to go after mine. Forever you will be the Romy to my Michelle and I love you forever and a day past that!

To my GFF, Lottie. No matter how much time lapses between us, "you and me us never part". Thank you for being the crazy uncensored you that you are. You too are another that tells me what I need to hear and not what I want to hear. Thank you for always having a big mouth, whether you right or not. I love that you are you. Time has nothing on the bond we share. We could go a million years without laying eyes on each other and I know the love and friendship would still be there. Stay who you are, don't ever change. And when it is time, God will do what He needs to do to use His "wild child" for His glory. Love you Chick!

To my aunts and uncles, you all played a detriment part in my upbringing. Although there were times when things escaped even your eyes, you all did an awesome job with your children and all your nieces and nephews. We don't say it enough, but I LOVE EACH AND EVERY ONE OF YOU! Aunt Debbie and Aunt Joyce, thank you for opening your doors and taking me in back then and trying to steer me the right way. It wasn't your fault it did not work. I just was not ready. You did the best you could. Aunt Sand, I still can't say thank you enough for taking in my kids when I experienced my Post-Partum Stress after the birth of Kai. THANK YOU.

To my son's father and step mother. YOU GUYS ROCK. You did an outstanding job with raising our son. Jas, to take on the responsibility of motherhood before you even have your own child is not an easy task and for that I say THANK YOU.

I must shout out some people that have been there and I know will still be there no matter where the journey takes me, I know no matter what it is, when I call, you coming and if you can't you sending somebody…lol: Dominique Burnette, Amanda Herd, Terri Terrell, Candace Elliot, My MC, Angela Tate, Quateria McGirt, LeKonda Rich, Ebony Rowland, Valerie Haywood, Helen Judd, Tiara Judd, Mama Reverend Mary Turner, Ashley Ratliff, and Angie White…. You are just a few that have weathered some storms with me as well. Thank you for your love.

I have one billion, three million, and four hundred gazillion cousins it seems like. I cannot name you all, but I love you all. I love you and I pray that as your gift makes room for you, that you give it back to God to use for His perfect will. You all were my first friends and I would not know what it meant to use my imagination had it not been for you all. Some of you are going to laugh and cry at remembering when these events took place and some of you might be like "where was I"? But all in all, you all play important parts in my life.

Shout out to my hairstylist, Melony at Salon 360 of Apex, NC. We have truly been through the fire and back, but I thank God for you Fam. You have always been the same and your heart is truly one of the biggest. I pray God grants you much success. I thank God that our paths led to forgiveness of the hurt between us and I look forward to many new funny memories being made with you. Love you!

Author Alvetta Rolle, if it had not been for your obedience that night when God laid it on your heart to reach out to me, this book would not be out right now. Thank you for your encouragement and for your awesome example!!! I pray that everything you think your career will do, that God exceeds it.

To my friend Corneal Sevyn Johnson also known as just "Seven". He Said to my She Said. You have inspired me so much since God placed you in my life. Thank you for showing us that there are some good ones out there and not just in our own personal inner circles. You know more than anyone the journey that God takes us on to get us on {think about it} and I thank you for your cheers. Your openness has encouraged not only me but countless others and I am glad I have a front row seat to seeing God complete that which He started in you.

A special thank you goes to Shelia Wilson and the Warm Lyrics Café family. You gave me my first opportunity to stand before people and share "By His Stripes". Before eyes even laid eyes on the finished copy, you were standing in support of this testimony and I thank you for that!

Last but not least, I have to thank my publishing family. Minister Paul Ellis and Shifting a Generation Publishing Company (Ellis & Ellis Consulting Group). Thank you. Thank you for allowing God to use you to give this opportunity. Thank you for being a door for His people to use to minister through their written words. I can only imagine how mad the enemy is at you for your obedience but I also know without a doubt that God will bless you with double for your trouble. Thank you and I look forward to a very long relationship with you all.

To anyone that I did not name personally, know that you are loved and your impact on my life is not taken lightly. I thank my grandparents and great grandparents for their hand in my life and for the prayers of the elders over me.

God Bless Each and Every One of You!

About

SILENT SINS IN THE CHURCH

Founded by Pastor Gwendolyn C. Scott of Raleigh, NC, Silent Sins in the Church Ministry is dedicated to the unspoken sin of domestic violence and sexual assault that women and men alike suffer in silence because they are afraid to speak out.

"An angry man stirs up dissension, and a hot tempered one commits many sins" –Proverbs 29:22

Admitting your sins in already hard enough in itself, but being a member of a church can make it even harder. The church community in the past has swept this very controversial topic under the carpet making it something which was just unspoken of. Often times than not, whether it is clergy, the gatekeeper, or someone in between, congregations are affected but choose to remain silent for the sake of "image".

The Book of Ecclesiastes tells us that there is a time for everything. Chapter 3 verse 7 tells us that "there is a time to tear and a time to mend, a time to be silent and a time to speak". Domestic violence is definitely a time to speak and with Silent Sins in the Church, that mission is being accomplished by the grace of God.

Pastor Gwendolyn Scott has over eighteen years' experience and training through Interact, an organization that advocates for victims of domestic violence, as well as with the North Carolina Department of Corrections. It is with this training and the anointing that God has placed within her that more than qualifies her to minister to those affected and that suffer in silence.

Christina Mial was taken under Pastor Gwendolyn's wing and began receiving mentoring to work with this ministry. Through her own healing from domestic violence and sexual assault, God began to show her how to use her pain for the purpose of healing His people. It was because of this relationship, that Silent Sins in the Church conferences were born. TrueWay Apostolic Ministries of Apex, NC holds an annual event in which women, men, and children can come to be empowered, edified, and educated on the topics domestic violence and sexual assault. Families receive resources, survivors' share stories, victims are remembered that have lost their lives, and souls are fed spiritually and naturally while being healed and learning the true gift of forgiveness.

To find out more about Silent Sins in the Church or to host a conference at your church, feel free to send an email to info@christinamial.com with the subject line SILENT SINS.

Finding Help to Heal in the Word of God

In Need of Healing/Coming Into a Storm In Life:

Psalm 34:17-20 *"The righteous cry out, and the LORD hears them; He delivers them from all their troubles. The LORD is close to the brokenhearted and saves those who are crushed in spirit."*

2 Corinthians 1:10 *"He has delivered us from such a deadly peril and He will deliver us. On Him we have set our hope that He will continue to deliver us."*

James 1:12 *"Blessed is the man who perseveres under trial, because when he has stood the test, he will receive the crown of life that God has promised to those that love Him."*

Psalm 119:75-76 *"I know, Oh LORD, that Your laws are righteous, and in faithfulness You have afflicted me. May Your unfailing love be my comfort, according to Your promise to Your servant."*

James 1:2-4 *"Consider it pure joy, my brothers, whenever you face trials of many kinds, because you know that the testing of your faith develops perseverance. Perseverance must finish its work so that you may be mature and complete, not lacking anything."*

Deuteronomy 31:6 *"Be strong and courageous. Do not be afraid or terrified because of them, for the LORD your God goes with you; He will never leave you nor forsake you."*

In the Midst of Waiting For the Answer/ The Eye of the Storm:

Proverbs 3:5-6 *"Trust in the LORD with all your heart and lean not on your own understanding; in all your ways acknowledge Him, and He will make your paths straight."*

Isaiah 55:6 *"Seek the LORD while He may be found; call on Him while He is near."*

Psalm 42:5 *"Why are you downcast, Oh my soul? Why so disturbed within me? Put your hope in God, for I will yet praise Him, my Savior and my God."*

Matthew 8:23-27 *"Then He got into the boat and His disciples followed Him. Without warning, a furious storm came up on the lake, so that the waves swept over the boat. But Jesus was sleeping. The disciples went and woke Him saying, "Lord, save us! We're going to drown!" He replied, "You of little faith, why are you so afraid?" Then He got up and rebuked the winds and the waves, and it was completely calm. The men were amazed and asked, "What kind of man is this? Even the winds and the waves obey Him?""*

Psalm 91:1-16 *" He who dwells in the shelter of the Most High will rest in the shadow of the Almighty. I will say of the LORD, "He is my refuge and my fortress, my God in whom I trust." Surely He will save you from the fowler's snare and from the deadly pestilence. He will cover you with His feathers, and under His wings you will find refuge; His faithfulness will be your shield and rampart. You will not fear the terror of night, nor the arrow that flies by day, nor the pestilence that stalks in the darkness, nor the plague that destroys at midday. A thousand may fall at your side, ten thousand at your right hand, but it will not come near you. You will only observe with your eyes and see* the punishment of the wicked. If you make the Most High your dwelling, even the LORD who is my refuge, then no harm will befall you, no disaster will come near your tent. For He will command His angels concerning you to guard you in all your ways; they will lift you up in their hands, so that you will not strike your foot against a stone. You will tread upon the lion and the cobra; you will trample the great lion and the serpent. "Because he loves me", says the LORD, "I will rescue him; I will protect him, for he acknowledges My name. He will call upon Me and I will answer him. I will be with him in trouble. I will deliver him and honor him. With long life, will I satisfy him and show him My salvation.""

Isaiah 40:31 *"but those who hope in the LORD will renew their strength. They will soar on wings like eagles; they will run and not grow weary; they will walk and not be faint."*

2 Corinthians 12:9 *"But He said to me, "My grace is sufficient for you, for My power is made perfect in weakness." Therefore I will boast all the more gladly about my weakness, so that Christ's power may rest on me."*

Jeremiah 30:17 *"But I will restore you to health and heal your wounds", declares the LORD, "because you are called an outcast, Zion for whom no one cares."*

When You're Healed/Coming Out of the Storm:

Psalm 3:4 *"To the LORD I cry aloud, and He answers me from His holy hill."*

Psalm 66:17-20 *"I cried out to Him with my mouth; His praise was on my tongue. If I had cherished sin in my heart, the Lord would not have listened; but God has surely listened and heard my voice in prayer. Praise be to God, who has not rejected my prayer or withheld His love from me."*

Colossians 1:13-14 *"For He has rescued us from the dominion of darkness and brought us into the kingdom of the Son He loves, in whom we have redemption, the forgiveness of sins."*

Romans 8:28 *"And we know that in all things God works for the good of those who love Him, who have been called, according to His purpose."*

Nahum 1:7 *"The LORD is good, a refuge in times of trouble. He cares for those who trust in Him"*

Hebrews 7:25 *"Therefore He is able to save completely those who come to God through Him, because He always lives to intercede for them."*

Acts 13:38-39 *"Therefore my brothers, I want you to know that through Jesus the forgiveness of sins is proclaimed to you. Through Him everyone who believes is justified from everything you could not be justified from by the law of Moses."*

Psalm 34:19-20 *"A righteous man may have many troubles, but the LORD delivers him from them all; He protects all his bones, not one of them will be broken."*

May there be something in these scriptures that encourages you as you push through your storms to your breakthroughs and to your healing of whatever ails you.

North Carolina Coalition Against Domestic Violence

Mission

The mission of the NCCADV is to create social change through the elimination of the institutional, cultural, and individual oppressions that contribute to domestic violence.

Vision

To empower all North Carolina communities to build a society that prevents and eliminates domestic violence.

Values

We believe that domestic violence is a pattern of domination in which perpetrators intentionally choose to cause fear, injury, and/or pain in order to gain and maintain power and control over their partners. In addition to physical violence, abuse can be sexual, emotional, economic, and can include stalking. We know that most domestic violence is committed by men and is a form of violence against women. We believe that domestic violence is absolutely unacceptable and that perpetrators should be held accountable.

We believe that patriarchy, gender, inequality, and all oppressions play a central role at the individual, institutional, and cultural levels in creating and maintaining an environment which accepts domestic violence. We believe it is vital to understand and advocate for the elimination of all forms of oppression, including but not limited to: racism, sexism, and homophobia. We believe it is critical to serve all domestic violence survivors regardless of race, age, class, ethnic group, sexual orientation, gender, identity, mental and physical abilities, religious and spiritual beliefs, and immigration status.

Every purchase of this book will help out the NCCADV in the form of $1.00 that I will donate to help them continue their work for this cause. You purchase will help with funding for education and resources that are needed to continue to empower and educate society on the issues of domestic violence.

To find out more on the NCCADV, visit their website at www.nccadv.org

Made in the USA
Charleston, SC
05 December 2013